Walter Edward Smith

**The recent depression of trade**

Its nature, its causes, and the remedies which have been suggested for it

Walter Edward Smith

**The recent depression of trade**
*Its nature, its causes, and the remedies which have been suggested for it*

ISBN/EAN: 9783337142896

Printed in Europe, USA, Canada, Australia, Japan

Cover: Foto ©Suzi / pixelio.de

More available books at **www.hansebooks.com**

# THE RECENT
# DEPRESSION OF TRADE

*ITS NATURE, ITS CAUSES, AND THE REMEDIES
WHICH HAVE BEEN SUGGESTED FOR IT*

BY

## WALTER E. SMITH

B.A. NEW COLLEGE

BEING THE OXFORD COBDEN PRIZE ESSAY FOR 1879

> "Wreck'd on a reef of visionary gold"
> TENNYSON

LONDON:
TRÜBNER AND CO., LUDGATE HILL.
JAMES THORNTON, HIGH STREET, OXFORD.
1880.
*All rights reserved.*

# PREFACE.

This Essay was originally sent in to the Registrar of the University of Oxford on May 3, 1879. It has now been carefully revised, and brought up to date—in parts entirely rewritten.

PUTNEY, *Feb. 26th,* 1880.

# CONTENTS.

### CHAPTER I.

|  | PAGE |
|---|---|
| INTRODUCTORY . . . . . . . . . . | 1 |

### CHAPTER II.

| WHAT IS THE NATURE OF THE DEPRESSION OF TRADE ? . . . . . . . . . . | 15 |
|---|---|

### CHAPTER III.

| THE CAUSES WHICH GAVE RISE TO THE DEPRESSION AT HOME . . . . . . . . | 39 |
|---|---|

### CHAPTER IV.

| THE CAUSES WHICH GAVE RISE TO THE DEPRESSION ABROAD . . . . . . . . . | 68 |
|---|---|

### CHAPTER V.

| REMEDIES PROPOSED FOR THE DEPRESSION . . | 82 |
|---|---|

# THE
# RECENT DEPRESSION OF TRADE.

## CHAPTER I.

**ERRATUM.**
*P.* 102, *line* 1, *for* "overvalued," *read* "undervalued."

astronomy than to the vastly complicated affairs of social life. We have just passed through a period of depression, which, though it came in perfect agreement with all past experience, was complicated by such an exceptional conglomeration of untoward circumstances, and protracted to such a weary length, that men seemed to lose faith in the revival which was almost certain to come sooner or later; and began to ask whether the commercial supremacy of this country was not permanently undermined. So weak was the faith of the public that when the revival seemed to be

# THE RECENT DEPRESSION OF TRADE.

## CHAPTER I.

### INTRODUCTORY.

IT has often been remarked that periods of depression and inflation of trade have for a long time alternated in a decennial cycle, with a regularity which is almost startling, and which seems more appropriate to the phenomena of astronomy than to the vastly complicated affairs of social life. We have just passed through a period of depression, which, though it came in perfect agreement with all past experience, was complicated by such an exceptional conglomeration of untoward circumstances, and protracted to such a weary length, that men seemed to lose faith in the revival which was almost certain to come sooner or later; and began to ask whether the commercial supremacy of this country was not permanently undermined. So weak was the faith of the public that when the revival seemed to be really beginning the *Times* took credit to itself for almost superhuman foresight, because it had always thought the depression would not last for ever! And now with the new decade the revival is really here.

We need have no fear of reaction now. We have during five or six years of weary dulness, paid the full penalty of the sins of the past inflation; and now, in spite of the miserable harvest of last year, which must have acted as a powerful drag upon returning prosperity, we are ready for a new period of inflated trade, of wild speculation, of rapid fortune making, and we are ready also to sow the seeds for a harvest of depression, bankruptcy, and misery which will be surely reaped in the later years of this new decade.

Let it not be supposed that in thus venturing upon prophecy I am indulging in vague conjecture, and a general belief that because the decennial period has prevailed in the past it will be repeated in the future. I write thus because I see that the same causes which have been so potent in the past will inevitably bring about similar results in the near future. Excessive railway making was among the most powerful of the causes which produced the inflation of 1870 and the following years, and which so impoverished the world that since then it has been sitting in poverty; and there is abundant evidence that we are just entering upon a new period of spasmodic railway speculation in almost every country of the world, which must produce the same effects that have always attended such a course.

This essay was originally written in the spring of 1879, at the very time when the depression reached its culminating point—the hour of greatest darkness and cold which precedes the day.

In America, indeed, there were, as I then pointed out, distinct traces of the approaching revival, but in England there was as yet no appearance of change. Now things are very different; our iron works are in full swing, thanks to a demand in America which the American furnaces are quite insufficient to supply, and no doubt our difficulties will soon have completely passed away.

But in spite of this change of circumstances, my essay has not become obsolete; nay, if there be any truth in the doctrines which I have maintained, now is the time when they should be listened to and laid to heart. I have insisted that it is in the sins of the time of the inflation that we must seek for the origin of the depression which follows as surely as the shadow follows the sunlight; whilst it is the forced economy of the depression which supplies material for the wild festivities of the inflation. I cannot expect much attention to my words from "those that eddy round and round;" but this time, if any, is the most suitable for my sermon, before men have forgotten the grinding lessons of adversity, and before they have once more committed the errors which will plunge them into fresh misery.

I propose to give some account of the nature of the depression from which we have just emerged, and of the causes which led to it. This latter question will have a direct practical bearing, since we can only escape or mitigate the recurrence of like effects, by avoiding to our utmost the mistakes which we then made. Unfortunately this remedy depends more upon the good sense and self-control of individuals, than on any course of action open to either legislature or government; hence we cannot look with sanguine hopes for any essential reform.

During the years which followed the Civil War in the United States, there arose in that country an extravagant and abnormal expenditure upon railways. This, combined with many other causes, produced a great inflation in the trade of the world, and especially of England. During the years 1871, 1872, and 1873 we appeared to be in the greatest prosperity. The prices of coal and iron in particular rose to an extravagant height. Every manufacturer and every trader was eager to extend his business to the utmost, and seemed to be rapidly making his fortune.

In the autumn of 1873 came the American railway panic which brought railway construction there to an abrupt standstill, and ushered in a period of depression and distress in commerce, manufactures, and agriculture, which steadily and continuously increased in intensity and extent from that time till the summer of last year. Trade then reached its lowest ebb, and since that time the tide has been rapidly rising. But, as the current of a river continues to flow down after the level of the water has begun to rise, so, although trade is improving rapidly, the revenue has hardly yet reached its lowest point.

Our depression largely arose from that in America, and it was the revival in America which gave the first token of returning animation in trade, and it has been mainly the strong American demand for iron which has infused fresh life into our markets.

In 1872 the exports of British produce reached their culminating point. Since that date they have been steadily shrinking in value from year to year without a single break, and have now fallen off 64¾ millions, or more than 25 per cent. But latterly the shrinkage of our imports has been even more marked than that of our exports, so that the "balance of trade" against us has become somewhat less. This result ought to be highly satisfactory to those practical men who think that the net gain of trade is to be measured by balancing the imports against the exports; but to others it was not altogether pleasing to find that our spending power was diminishing even more rapidly than our export trade.

The decrease in value of our exports was mainly—according to some authorities\* almost entirely—due to a general fall in prices, caused perhaps by a rise in the value of gold. Now this shrinkage in value has involved great and often ruinous loss to the capitalist, to whom the past six years have been a time of severe and growing difficulty. The following picture of the recent state of affairs, though perhaps an exaggeration, is by no means too gross an exaggeration to be worth quoting:—
"We shall not be very far wrong in saying that the great bulk of the commercial capital employed in the manufacturing and distributing trades has yielded scarcely any interest at all for three years, and during the last year there have been severe losses."

A natural result of this disastrous state of

---

\* See Mr. Giffen's "Report on the Prices of Exports of British and Irish Produce in the years 1861-77."

trade may be traced in the great number of failures which have occurred of late, and especially in the gigantic and disgraceful failure of the City of Glasgow Bank. It is perhaps hardly possible that any degree of reckless and dishonest banking should have piled up so vast a debt as that bank had incurred, unless it had been helped by losses of a more legitimate character. The number of trade failures of minor importance was very large; some were of a most discreditable kind. For instance, the creditors of one firm agreed to accept a composition of $1\frac{1}{4}d.$ in the £! Many, however, succumbed who could not be charged with dishonest or even speculative trading.

It would be easy to accumulate evidence to prove the great losses to which capitalists have of late been subjected. The facts, however, are so notorious that it is unnecessary now to fill up space with illustrations of a state of things which has happily passed, or is passing away.

The very low rates of interest for the loan of money which prevailed for several years are a strong proof that there was but little profit to be made with it. For a long time two per cent. was the usual bank rate of discount; a fact which shows that the rate of the open market for good securities was still lower. It is certain that this arose not from any large supply of capital, but from an extreme weakness of demand, arising from the impossibility of employing it profitably, or of finding adequate security.

The leading industries of the country, especially those in iron and cotton, were in a miserable state of prostration. In a circular addressed last spring to the owners of Scotch mines by thirteen leading iron-masters, we find the following statement :—" It is a fact that the selling price of Scotch pig-iron has for some time been considerably under the price of production, and it is no secret that the Scotch iron-masters during the last twelve or eighteen months have been working at a heavy loss."

It is notorious that the shipping business, which is at once in itself an important factor of our trade, and also a good index of the state of other trades, was in a most languishing condition. The navigation returns do not, indeed, show any falling off in tonnage; but it was precisely the impossibility of suddenly diminishing the tonnage employed which added so seriously to the difficulties of shipowners. For several years freight was so excessively low that many ships have lain for months in harbour, their owners finding that course less expensive than to send them on voyages.

The demand for iron steamships has probably

never been feebler; certainly their price was never lower than in the early part of last year.

This apparent decay in our exports necessarily roused the gravest solicitude, and the most anxious inquiries whether it were real or apparent, temporary or permanent.

Thanks to Free Trade more than to any other cause we have placed ourselves in a position occupied by no other nation. We have devoted ourselves mainly to the production of iron, cotton, coal, and other goods which we cannot eat. We *must* exchange them for foreign corn and meat or we die, for we usually draw about a third of our corn supply from abroad, and in years of deficient harvest a still larger part. Our population is so greatly increased through our manufactures and our trade* that it could not be supported on the produce of British fields. " If England were cut off from all foreign trade, a large portion of her people must surely perish, as surely as did more than a million of Irish, when the potato disease left them foodless on the land."†

While industry and trade have suffered thus deeply, the plight of agriculture has been perhaps

---

\* Between 1801 and 1871 the population of England and Wales increased from 8,892,536 to 22,712,266.

† Professor Bonamy Price, *Contemporary Review*, April, 1877.

yet worse. A succession of five bad harvests, the aggregate loss upon which we must reckon at considerably over 100 millions sterling, in conjunction with the low prices at which agricultural produce has been selling, has reduced the most prosperous farmers to distress. A new feature in their difficulty is that the large supplies of food imported from abroad have deprived them of what Lord Beaconsfield justly called "the somewhat dismal compensation of high prices." The loss primarily falls upon the the farmers, but is now passing over to the land-owners, who have much difficulty in finding tenants for their farms, even at reduced rents. The quantity of land under cereal cultivation has shown a diminution of more than 10 per cent. since 1869.\*

Nor has the depression been confined to England. It has affected almost the whole of the civilized world. The United States in particular have suffered far more than we. Mr. John Bright writes of America,† "The distress during the last five years has been far more prolonged, more widely spread, and far more intense than in this country." It is true that our imports from the United States have more than doubled in the

---

\* The acreage of corn crops in the United Kingdom reached its maximum, i.e., 12,000,111 in 1869. In 1879 it was 10,777,000.
† In a Letter, dated April 1, 1879.

last nine years.* We shall, however, see presently that the rapid growth of exports from America, as in the parallel case of Germany, is, with respect to manufactures, a morbid growth, which does not indicate true prosperity.

Perhaps (in spite of the doctrines of " practical men," and of the newspapers) we shall find a truer index to the real prosperity of America in her imports than in her exports. Her total imports for home consumption have sunk since 1873 from 130 millions to 88 millions, which was their value in 1878. This is a decrease of $32\frac{1}{3}$ per cent. No doubt this falling off is in a great measure due to the direct effect of protection, but it also implies an immense diminution of spending power. In America, the commercial distress has been greatly aggravated by the exorbitant prices produced by a " barbarous" protective tariff. This tariff is one of the legacies of the American Civil War. The American manufacturers finding their country burdened with debt, and in need of a large revenue, were delighted at the opportunity afforded them of introducing a monstrous tariff.

Hence, it is not the capitalist only who has suffered there. The distress has affected all

---

* In 1869 they were valued at $42\frac{1}{2}$ millions, and in 1878 at 89 millions.

classes, including even the farmers, whose competition is so much dreaded by their English rivals. They are in the unfortunate position of losing everything and gaining nothing, not even seeming to gain anything by protection. The manufacturers, who in spite of their extravagant tariff, ranging up to 275 per cent. on the value,* are unable entirely to monopolise the market at home, and utterly unable to compete profitably abroad, are constantly crying out for more and more protection, and generally get it. We may find a striking proof of American distress in the emigration returns. The stream of emigrants to America was greatly checked for awhile. The net total of immigrants thither, that is, the excess of immigrants over emigrants reached a maximum of more than 400 thousand in 1872, and in 1877 had sunk to 70 thousand. The number of emigrants of British origin to the United States in 1876 was 143 *less* than the number of those who returned thence. However, the tide has turned once more, and the excess of emigrants over immigrants of British origin was 603 in 1877 and 20,654 in 1878. Americans sometimes speak of the " pauper's" wages to be earned in Europe, but the working

---

\* See the valuable Table of Foreign Tariffs prepared by a Committee of the Wolverhampton Chamber of Commerce.

classes were finding out that for the present they were worse off there than here.

Nor are the nations of Europe in better plight. Turn where we will, we find nothing but stagnation and distress. France, perhaps, "the heroine of Political Economy," has suffered less seriously than any other country in spite of the heavy burden which was laid upon her by the war.

In consequence of this state of general impoverishment there has been much discussion as to the causes which have led to our trouble, coupled with proposals for measures of relief, which are too often either impracticable or positively hurtful. In particular, the faith in free trade, which till lately seemed so firmly rooted in the mind of every Englishman, has been shaken, and a cry for protection, concealed under the specious name of reciprocity, was raised so loudly as to excite some alarm, not that we should be false to our free trade principles— for such apostasy is rendered almost impossible by our circumstances—but that the question which had seemed for ever settled in this country would be re-opened, and once more seriously debated.

"Reciprocity" was the most dangerous nostrum which was proposed for the depression of trade; however, we shall have to consider one or two others, and especially to examine the view of those who believe that by some alteration in the currency, which measures and distributes goods, they can cure the most deep-seated evils in the economy of the world.

## CHAPTER II.

#### WHAT IS THE NATURE OF THE DEPRESSION OF TRADE?

BEFORE we consider the causes which have led to the depression under which we have been labouring, it will be well to try to arrive at a clear understanding of the nature of the phenomenon in question.

There is an abuse of language which we sometimes meet with, for the most part in newspapers; we hear of a "crisis" which has been going on for the last six years. This seems to betray some confusion of idea between depression of trade and an entirely different phenomenon, a "crisis" or a "panic" in the city when merchants are in agony for the loan of money and cannot get it. It does not require any profound analysis to see the utter unlikeness of this to a period of commercial depression, such as we have passed through, in which the greatest difficulty is experienced in lending money at all.

There is, however, another distinction to be drawn, less obvious, and therefore more important. We shall endeavour to show that under the name " commercial depression" are confused together two phenomena closely connected in their causes, but distinct in their effects.

And first we must draw a wide distinction between the processes of production and consumption of wealth on the one hand, and its distribution on the other. The two first, opposite as they are in their nature and their effects, may naturally be grouped together on account of their marked opposition to the process of distribution. They have this in common that they alter the sum total of wealth in the world, and that any failure in production, or excess in consumption, impoverishes the whole world by so much. With distribution it is different. In considering questions of distribution, we assume that the goods are already in existence, and merely have to decide how they are to be shared.

Now, it is obvious that the total wealth and the general well-being of the world depend indirectly on the processes of distribution no less than on those of production and consumption. It is hardly necessary to illustrate the fact that one method of distribution is more favourable to production than another, or that one is more likely to encourage over-expenditure than another, but the fact on which I would now lay stress is, that distribution is a great department of human activity which does not immediately affect the sum total of human wealth at all. No kind of gambling, no rise or fall in prices, no panic in the city can directly make the world either richer or poorer. In all these things, what one man loses another gains. It is only by producing that the world is made richer, and by consuming that it is made poorer.

Gold has often been imagined to be wealth in a very peculiar sense. In truth it is in a very peculiar sense not wealth; for though in itself it is a costly and valuable article, it is not generally used as such, but simply as a guarantee, and with no direct reference to its physical properties. In this case it merely forms part of the machinery of distribution, of the counters by which wealth is measured and exchanged. That this is so may be seen from the fact that a piece of paper will often answer precisely the same purposes as a piece of gold.

Now, when trade is in a state of depression, we may mean either that the machinery of production and consumption is out of order, or we may mean merely that there is some fault in distribution, and that it is in such a state as to benefit one class of the community at the expense of another; and of this we may be tolerably sure, that the class which is suffering will have a far clearer idea of its own condition, and will make itself heard far more loudly than the class which is prospering. Adam Smith tells us that " When profits are diminished, merchants are very apt to complain that trade decays; though the diminution of the profits is the natural effect of prosperity, or of a greater stock being employed in it than before."

There are many indications which suggest the conclusion that during the earlier years of the depression there was no material diminution in the quantities produced, and consequently no general suffering among the working classes. Prices were depressed and so the capitalists got a smaller, and the workman a larger share of the things produced than before. In 1877 and 1878 the nature of the depression seems to have undergone a gradual change. The quantities produced, as well as the prices, fell off, and the working classes as well as the capitalists have suffered deeply. The capitalist naturally imagines that when he is making little or no profits the whole nation is in a wretched state of poverty, but to those who think most of the happiness of the great mass of the people, it will be far from an unmixed sorrow to see the capitalist losing, if only his loss prove to be the workman's gain. About 24,000,000 out of our population of 34,000,000 are included among the labouring classes.* It is to these we should

---

* See Professor Leone Levi's letter to Mr. Bass, Jan. 2, 1879.

mainly look in estimating the happiness and prosperity of the country at large, not only because of their numbers, but also because to them a little gain or loss generally means much more in the way of personal comfort or misery than to those who have more luxuries to give up.* Professor Fawcett points out that during the inflation in the prices of coal and iron in 1872, an enormous tax was laid on the people of England, not only on their consumption of coal and iron, but also on that of all goods made with coal and iron, for the benefit of the fortunate owners and lessees of coal mines. Now we can afford to see this tax reduced with great equanimity, even though coal-owners seemed not to be the only persons who shared in the general prosperity.

Prices fell greatly, and this, since values are always measured by money, makes the wages of workmen appear to have fallen, even where they have really risen (in money's worth), and makes the profits of capitalists appear to have shrunk even more than they really have.

The main causes of this fall in prices seem to have been a general diminution in the demand for goods, owing to universal impoverishment, and a rise in the price of gold caused by a diminishing

---

\* "Free Trade and Protection," p. 138.

supply, as well as an increased demand abroad for purposes of coinage.

The chief effect of the weak demand for our goods seems for a long time to have been only to lower the prices we received for them, not to diminish the quantity which we produced. It is certain, at any rate, that the *volume* of our foreign exports did not fall off in the same degree as their *value*. Indeed, according to Mr. Giffen,[*] the exports of 1877 were very nearly equal in volume to those of 1873, and would come within a million pounds of their value if they were reckoned at the prices of 1873. According to other calculations, however, apparently most careful and trustworthy,[†] out of a difference in value of £54,960,000 between the exports[‡] of 1872 and 1877, £13,550,000 or 24·6 per cent. is due to a decrease in quantity, and £41,410,000 only to the fall in prices. This is a serious discrepancy which calls for remark and explanation, and warns us not to trust too implicitly to the results arrived at by statisticians. I shall not attempt to check these calculations, but may perhaps venture to remark that the results

---

[*] Report to the Secretary of the Board of Trade on the prices of exports of British and Irish produce in the years 1861–1875.

[†] *Economist*, July 27, 1878.

[‡] The exports taken into calculation both by Mr. Giffen and by the *Economist* are those exports only of British and Irish produce, whose value and quantity are both given in the Board o Trade returns.

of the *Economist* appear *primâ facie* the most probable.

We may remark parenthetically that the returns of exports and imports collected by the Board of Trade, especially with regard to the values, are estimated by the merchants, or the merchants' clerks, who supply them in such a perfunctory manner that it is impossible to found trustworthy and accurate conclusions upon them. Many stories are told in illustration of this. A certain chemical manufacturer, for instance, was in the habit for years of returning all dry chemicals which he exported, however valuable, under the heading of "ashes." Another merchant found it convenient to class all kinds of goods together indiscriminately under the title of "umbrellas." These were not dishonest falsifications of returns, they were merely a conventional method of saving trouble; but they may cause some perplexity to the unwary student of statistics.

So long as the diminution of demand is met by a fall of price and the quantity sold does not decrease, or does not materially decrease, the working classes will on the whole gain and the capitalist lose by a fall in prices and dull trade. The reason of this is simple enough. Workmen receive wages fixed in money for the time being, which wages, together with the other fixed charges, must come out of the price obtained for the goods made, before the *entrepreneur* (if we may borrow a convenient expression from Professor Walker) gets his profit, which is the surplus that is then left over.

Now, if the workman and the *entrepreneur* were always to receive the same share of the produce, the money wages of the former would have to fall in proportion to the price of the goods which he makes. If it were so arranged, and if all goods rose and fell in value equally, and if the retail price fell in proportion to the wholesale price (or, in other words, if we could eliminate all friction from our social machinery), the workman, though his money wages might fall, would not in reality be affected by the change. He might get ten shillings instead of twenty shillings, but he could buy as much in goods as formerly. Whilst if he had any savings in the bank they would be worth twice as much to him. But in truth there is far more "friction," and consequently more complexity, in the matter than we have supposed. If prices fall it is impossible for employers to reduce the money wages of their men in the same proportion. The skilled artisan may have to put up with a considerable reduction, but the commoner kinds of labour will certainly not suffer proportionate loss. The employer is not likely to recoup himself for a fall in prices out of the wages of his labourers, unless he is compelled to do so by seeing his profits sink so low that he has little choice; the weight of *vis inertiæ*, the dread of the Trades' Union and of strikes, the natural humanity of the master all combine to forbid it. Hence, we may be pretty sure that as long as the workman is kept in full employment he will receive as wages a larger share of the price of the articles he produces when that price is low than when it is high; though it may well happen that the money value of his share has shrunk.

Let us suppose for the sake of simplicity that the prices of all goods have fallen to half their former value, and that the labourer formerly got half the price of what he produced, and now gets three quarters. Thus, a man who formerly produced goods to the value of £2, and received £1 in wages, will now make goods to the value of £1 and get 15s. in wages. His money wages have sunk 5s., but he will be none the worse off, since the prices of all goods are at half their former rates; so he will be able to buy with his 15s. half as much again as he formerly would with his £1.

Of course, as a matter of fact, prices do not all fall equally. The coal miner, though his wages have not fallen nearly in proportion to the price of coal (because they did not rise in proportion to it during the years of inflation), is much worse off now than he was, because his wages have fallen more than the prices of the things he buys.

Still our illustration shows how on an average, and in general, the workman gains by low prices. It is conceivable, indeed, that where a nation is dependent as we are on foreign countries for its food, a fall in the price of home manufactures, not accompanied by a corresponding fall in the price of foreign food, might bring distress on the whole nation without any diminution of the quantity of the home produce. But it is clear that this was not the case with us, though it probably was with several foreign nations, the rise in value of whose exports we envy so much. The distressed farmer will bear witness that there has been no scarcity of cheap food in England.

The retail dealers are another class who gain by a fall in prices. Friction is always powerfully on their side, and enables them to filch from the consumer much of the advantage which he ought to derive from low prices. Every one knows how quickly the retailer discovers any rise in the price of the articles he sells, and how soon he recoups himself from his customers. We also know how slow he is (unless his perceptions are quickened by keen competition, especially by that of the hated Cooperative Stores) to discover any fall in the price of his goods.

On the other hand, in the case of a general rise of prices, it is the capitalist who makes high profits, and the working man who loses in real reward. It is true that "a brisk trade," that is to say, a high rate of profits and plenty of orders, encourages the employers to compete eagerly for labour, and not to be particular as to the wages they pay; hence it is sure to produce a rise in money wages; or even when some one trade is enjoying greater prosperity than the rest, it may in that particular trade cause a rise in real wages. But on an average it is certain that, thanks to "friction," the employers will get a larger share than before of the things produced; in other words, their *real* remuneration on an average will be greater in spite of the rise in prices, while that of the workmen will be less.

It appears, for instance, that during the coal inflation of 1872, when we read many complaints of miners who only worked three days a week, and indulged in champagne and pineapples (*vide* " Punch" *passim*), the miners in reality got a very small share of the enhanced price. It appears, for instance, from evidence collected by a Select Committee of the House of Commons\* that, "In the West of Yorkshire district, between October, 1871, and March, 1873, there was an advance in the price of coal at

---

\* Quoted by Professor Fawcett, " Free Trade and Protection," p. 138.

the pit's mouth of 15s. 5d. a ton, while wages in this period were advanced only 1s. 1½d. a ton."

But when the depression of trade is so severe that the quantities produced decrease as well as the price obtained, then it is very different in its nature. It affects production and not distribution only. Less is produced altogether, so that there is likely to be keen distress among the working classes as well as among the capitalists. The dividend is less, so all the quotients will be less; at any rate there will be great slackness of employment, and many will be thrown altogether out of work.

It is my belief that till 1878 the depression in trade was of the kind I have endeavoured to describe; one in which the nation as a whole was not losing, though the traders and manufacturers (who so easily mistake themselves for the whole nation) were suffering keenly.

There are various indications which strongly support this view. In the first place it is impossible to bring forward a stronger proof than is contained in a fact which has caused utter despair to the "practical" man. In spite of the depression of trade, and the miserable falling off of our exports, our imports rose in value with hardly any break till 1877, as we may see by the following table of our total imports expressed in millions sterling, also of our imports per head of population. The last column is, of course, of great importance in relation to the question of the general level of comfort.

|  | Total Imports. Millions of £ | Imports per head of population. £ s. d. |
|---|---|---|
| 1870 | 303 | 9 14 4 |
| 1871 | 331 | 10 10 1 |
| 1872 | 355 | 11 2 6 |
| 1873 | 371 | 11 11 2 |
| 1874 | 370 | 11 8 3 |
| 1875 | 374 | 11 8 5 |
| 1876 | 375 | 11 6 8 |
| 1877 | 394 | 11 15 10 |
| 1878 | 369 | 10 18 3 |
| 1879* | 362 | 0 12 0 |

The increase in the quantities must have been much greater than that of the values, having to a great extent counterbalanced and concealed the fall of prices. It is probable that the imports for 1877 and 1878 if they were valued at the prices which held in 1872 would be worth about 420 millions. (See the *Economist*, July 20, 1878, and January 18, 1879.)

Now, this steady growth of the imports, both in

---

\* It is perhaps worth while to remark that when this Essay was first written I inserted here a conjectural estimate for the year 1879, founded on the hypothesis that the decrease on the whole year would be in the same proportion as that on the first three months; the result so obtained was 323,000,000, which number by its contrast with the actual imports for the year, which amounted to 362,127,741, strikingly exhibits the improvement of trade which has since taken place.

value and in quantity, as well as of the imports per head of population, shows clearly that the comfort and material happiness of the mass of the people must have been steadily improving.

If we look at some of the items of import, we shall be confirmed in our belief that the inflation of 1870-1873 was mainly a capitalist's inflation, harmful to the working classes; whilst the depression from 1873 or 1874 to the beginning of 1878 was a capitalist's depression advantageous to the working classes. Professor Fawcett ("Free Trade and Protection," p. 136) justly remarks that "it is generally admitted that the quantity of tea which is annually consumed by the English people affords a very correct index of the prosperity of the country." It is distinctly a luxury. But it is the luxury of the whole people and not a few. Now, throughout these years of depression the tea imported and retained for consumption has shown a steady improvement, both in total quantity and (what is perhaps more important) in quantity per head of population. The following are the figures:—

Quantity of tea consumed per head of population in lbs.

| | | | | |
|---|---|---|---|---|
| 1870 | 3·81 | 1875 | 4·44 |
| 1871 | 3·92 | 1876 | 4·50 |
| 1872 | 4·01 | 1877 | 4·52 |
| 1873 | 4·11 | 1878 | 4·66 |
| 1874 | 4·23 | 1879 | 4·11 |

This seems to indicate a decided improvement in prosperity, though we must not forget one disturbing element. Tea, like beer, is a cheap beverage as compared with wine, and hence will be drunk more largely by the wealthier classes when they are badly off than when they are prospering.

The same remarks hold good of tobacco, which is more completely a luxury than tea, and cannot be used as a substitute for any more expensive article. In this case there is a steady increase till 1877, followed by a decided drop in 1878 and 1879. The figures per head of population are as follows:—

| | | | | |
|---|---|---|---|---|
| 1870 | ............ | 1·34 | 1875 | ............ | 1·46 |
| 1871 | ............ | 1·36 | 1876 | ............ | 1·47 |
| 1872 | ............ | 1·37 | 1877 | ............ | 1·49 |
| 1873 | ............ | 1·41 | 1878 | ............ | 1·45 |
| 1874 | ............ | 1·44 | 1879 | ............ | 1·42 |

The sudden diminution in consumption which took place in 1878 naturally suggests that the increased duty which was levied in that year was the cause of the diminished consumption. However, Sir Stafford Northcote, in his Budget speech of last year, argued—no doubt correctly—that this could not be so, as the price of tobacco had so fallen that it was cheaper than it had been before, in spite of the increased duty. Hence he inferred that the diminished consumption was due to diminished prosperity. It should be noticed that this diminution did not begin till 1878.

There are one or two other facts which we may cite in proof of our position that there was at first no general distress. Pauperism, for instance, showed a considerable diminution during the depression, until 1878. The total number of paupers in receipt of relief on the 1st January in England and Wales reached a maximum of 1,081,926 in 1871, since which year it declined continuously till 1877, when it stood 728,350. In 1878 it had risen again to 742,703, and in 1879 it stood at 800,426. The number of adult able-bodied paupers also stood at its lowest in January 1877, when it was 92,806. In 1878 it had increased to 97,927, and in 1879 to 118,933. An alarming increase of more than 28 per cent. in two years. It is, however, very noteworthy that the increase did not begin till 1877.

Again, the amount of the deposits in Savings Banks has shown no falling off, but, on the contrary, a steady increase.*

---

\* The deposits in the hands of Savings Banks in the United Kingdom at the end of each of the seven last years were as follows:—

| | | | | |
|---|---|---|---|---|
| 1872 | ............... | £59,406,687 | 1876 | ............... £70,280,120 |
| 1873 | ............... | 61,667,884 | 1877 | ............... 74,226,175 |
| 1874 | ............... | 64,663,418 | 1878 | ............... 75,966,626 |
| 1875 | ............... | 67,595,114 | | |

There is, indeed, one important series of figures which at first sight seems to contradict the conclusion at which we have arrived. The number of marriages has greatly decreased since the time of high water in our trade. It was greatest in 1873, and has decreased almost continuously since that time. The numbers for the United Kingdom are as follows :—

| | | | |
|---|---|---|---|
| 1873 | 258,615 | 1876 | 254,825 |
| 1874 | 252,738 | 1877 | 244,864 |
| 1875 | 251,170 | 1878 | 239,353 |

Thus the number of marriages since 1873 has, in spite of the growth of population, fallen off by more than 19,000, or about 7·4 per cent. 161 persons out of every 10,000 were married in 1873, and in 1878 only 141. It will be observed that though the decrease has taken place throughout the whole period of depression it has become much more marked during the last two years. Between 1873 and 1876 the diminution was only 3990. Between 1876 and 1878 it was 15,472. Moreover, the difference between 1873 and 1876, which is not great when we remember that it is a falling off from an abnormally high rate, does not necessarily indicate any real diminution of general prosperity in the country. People are encouraged to marry not by a careful calculation of their real means founded on the costs of housekeeping, but by the vague impression that they are in good employment and getting high wages. This impression, of course, would be very common in the years of prosperous and inflated trade, when money wages were high, although prices were still higher. People who wanted to marry did not calculate how low their real wages were, still less how hollow and transitory a thing was much of the apparent prosperity.

The marriage returns suggest, indeed, an important qualification which must be made when we assert that till 1878 the condition of the working man was improving. It did not seem to be improving. He is not a political economist, and like most other people reckons his income in money. If his money wages are reduced he feels aggrieved and does not think much about the price of corn. Nor is it a question of feeling only. If he thinks he is a loser he may strike, and a strike like a war, whether successful or unsuccessful, is an immense waste, and is almost certain to turn a fancied loss into a real and heavy one. We shall have more to say of strikes presently. This much by way of parenthesis, to show how deep an injury may be done indirectly to the working classes by a fall in money wages, even though it result from a still greater fall of prices.

The expression " balance is trade" is dangerous, for though in itself it has a distinct and valuable meaning, it is closely associated with the false and pernicious doctrine, called by Adam Smith the " mercantile system ;" the doctrine that a nation grows richer by its exports and poorer by its imports, and that the real profit of its trade is to be measured by the excess of the former over the latter. Not only is this theory false in itself, but it would be difficult to mention any false opinion which has in practice given rise to such pernicious results.

We will try to use the words and yet to steer clear of their evil associations. The "balance of trade," then, is the difference in value between the exports and imports of *merchandise*, whether between some particular country and the rest of the world, or between any two countries. It is clear that this balance must be paid in some form or other by the country "against" whom it stands. Now, it has often been noticed, with unreasoning alarm, that the balance of trade against us is very large, and has till of late been rapidly growing. In the seven years from 1865 to 1871 inclusive, the balance against us varied from 67 millions (in 1868) to $47\frac{1}{2}$ millions (in 1871), the average amount being about $55\frac{1}{2}$ millions. In 1872 the balance stood at the low sum of 40 millions, but since that year till 1877 it has rapidly increased, as we may see from the following table of total exports, total imports, and of the difference between them :—

|      | Exports. Millions of £ | Imports. Millions of £ | Balance. Millions of £ |
|------|------------------------|------------------------|------------------------|
| 1872 | 314                    | 354                    | 40                     |
| 1873 | 311                    | 371                    | 60                     |
| 1874 | 297                    | 370                    | 72                     |
| 1875 | 281                    | 374                    | 92                     |
| 1876 | 256                    | 375                    | 118                    |
| 1877 | 252                    | 394                    | 142                    |
| 1878 | 245                    | 368                    | 123                    |

Thus, during five years from 1872 to 1877 the balance against us rose from 40 millions to 142 millions. In 1878 the tide turned, and the balance against us was considerably lessened, the imports having fallen off much more than the exports.

Now, it is natural and right that there should be a balance against us. We are the richest people in the world, and have invested our surplus capital abroad, both in public and private loans and in private undertakings, especially railways. Besides this there is a large number of Englishmen who are making money abroad, in India or in the colonies, who send remittances to their relatives in England,\* or who come home to spend the

---

\* The amount remitted home from the United States and Canada in 1878 is stated at £784,067. This return, however, does not profess to be complete.—"Statistical Tables relating to Emigration and Immigration in 1878."

fortunes which they have earned at the Antipodes; and our merchants do a large carrying trade for foreign countries, which in no way swells our own trade returns, but which is necessarily paid for in imports without corresponding exports. In all these ways we have an immense tribute continually coming in to us from abroad which must be sent to us in goods; at least the balance between what is thus due to us and the fresh capital which we lend out must ultimately come in that form.

There is another circumstance which makes the balance against us appear rather larger than it really is. The values given in our trade returns are estimated in England; so that, in the case of imports carriage is counted—with the exports it is not. Hence the "balance" is not struck fairly.

These considerations show why the balance of trade is normally and constantly "against" us, but they do not explain why it increased so largely during the earlier years of the depression. It is certain that foreign countries have not been sending us their produce for nothing, and yet we have not fully paid them in goods. Nor has the balance been set right in gold and silver. In these metals, as in other merchandise, there has been a considerable balance against us,* which has to be

---

* In our use of the word "against" of the balance in precious metals, we are speaking after the analogy—but by no means in the spirit—of the "commercial system."

added to that arising from ordinary trade. In each of the last six years our imports of gold and silver have considerably exceeded our exports except in 1877, when the exports were rather the greater.

From 1873 to 1878 we have imported gold and silver in excess of our exports to the aggregate value of 28½ millions—that is to say, on an average of 4¾ millions a year. These figures ought to bring much comfort to those who believe that the wealth of a nation consists in its gold and silver. To those who know that these are only two out of many objects of trade, and that every country is sure to import as much of them as it has need for, the above figures will be of interest only as a confirmation of their previous conviction.

Nor have we redressed the balance by running into debt; the debts owed by England to foreigners are insignificant when compared with those which are owed to us. But we have, for the most part, ceased to lend abroad, partly because we have found that many of our debtors are utterly untrustworthy (and certainly no one can regret that we have ceased to lavish our wealth upon Turkey and Paraguay, upon Egypt and Ecuador), partly also because our capitalists have so little to lend. Moreover, the contrary process has for the time set in. We have been calling in our old debts because the capitalist has been losing heavily and has been obliged to sell out securities. The working man who has gained so much of what the capitalist lost, did not care for the securities, but preferred to spend them on meat and corn and beer. Hence we have bought cargoes of provisions from America and have paid for them in railway shares and government stocks. If the working classes had been losing like their employers we should have had no occasion for the foreign goods.

The fact that the imports last year greatly fell off as well as the exports, and that the balance of trade against us was thus diminished, was cold comfort in our distress. It was not a sign that we were saving more, only that we had less to spend. The capitalist was losing more heavily than ever, and the workman was no longer gaining all that the capitalist lost.

So far we have considered the effects of a depression of trade on capital and labour respectively. It is well to remark before concluding this chapter that there is a large minority of the nation who gain greatly and obviously by depressed trade and low prices. These are all those whose income is fixed in money, whether they belong to any branch of the Queen's service, or hold some other office of which the remuneration is invariable, or draw their income from fixed investments, such as government stocks, mortgages, preference shares, and the like, or enjoy fixed annuities of any other kind, such as pensions or charges upon estates. To all such persons (and amongst their number are many who deserve our deepest sympathy, the widow, the orphan, the helpless) brisk trade and a rise in prices are an unmixed evil.

## CHAPTER III.

### THE CAUSES WHICH GAVE RISE TO THE DEPRESSION AT HOME.

THE causes of the depression of trade in England naturally fall under two great heads.

The whole world was impoverished by consuming too much and producing too little, and could not afford to buy our iron and cotton. If we survey the nations of the world we shall find that they have almost all, in one way or another, been consuming more than they have been producing, and this with nations no less than with individual men is the certain road to poverty and ruin.

But it is also true that various causes have combined to diminish the share of the world's work which we do, and to make it less than that for which we have provided the factories and the furnaces.

It will be convenient first to consider why we suffered more than our neighbours from the general impoverishment of the world, and then to consider the causes which led to that impoverishment.

The export trade of many other nations has fallen off, but in most cases to a less extent than ours; whilst that of Russia, the United States, and Germany, shows a considerable development.*

There are several causes which we may assign for the fact that England has lost more of the world's custom than her neighbours. In the first place, during the period of prosperity her trade and manufactures were inflated to a thoroughly abnormal extent. The main causes of this excessive inflation I will try to enumerate.

1. The Franco-German War.

It is clear that the enormous armies brought into the field on both sides were not only a great direct loss to the industry of their own countries, but were also consumers of produce on a large scale; so that at the very moment when their consumption

---

* The exports from Russia in 1877 had increased 52·7 per cent. since the years 1872 and 1873. Those of the United States had increased 56·6 per cent. in 1878. The values of the German exports are not given, but from the almost universal increase in the quantities, there can be no doubt that the total value has also increased. The British exports of home produce in the same periods fell off 22·2 and 24·5 per cent. respectively. With respect to Germany we must remember that in the years 1872 and 1873 she was recovering from the effects of the war with France, which, economically speaking, was not less disastrous to her than to her adversary.

was largest their powers of production were paralyzed. The ultimate result was that the nations concerned were greatly impoverished and have become bad customers to us; but for the moment our industry and commerce were powerfully stimulated.

2. We have already alluded to the railway mania which seized upon the United States after the civil war had been brought to a close. The whole nation seemed to be engaged in making railways and in making their fortune. In eight years (from January 1, 1865, to January 1, 1873) the American railway system was doubled in mileage. It had increased from 35,000 miles to upwards of 70,000.\* In the course of four consecutive years (1869-1872) 24,305 miles of railway were opened—that is to say, an average of over 6000 miles a year. For a considerable time America was spending over 100 millions every year upon railways.

The speculative tendencies of the Americans which doubtless were strong enough already were fanned to a flame by unwise legislation which set a premium upon premature railway making, in the form of land grants conditional on the lines being opened by specified dates. Hence there arose an extraordinary inflation, as in England,

---

\* Poor's "American Railway Manual."

followed by a panic and extraordinary depression. This result was natural. The whole nation had been devoting its energies and its wealth (and much of our wealth too) to the making of railroads through the desert which, though in time they will be very useful, cannot repay their cost for many years. A population must first grow up around them. In the meanwhile they have impoverished the nation as effectually as if it had spent its millions in the erection of pyramids.

England, of course, shared largely in this hollow prosperity. There was an immense demand for English capital and English iron which stimulated speculation and sent iron and coal up to famine prices, and which acted at the same time powerfully, though less directly, upon other branches of trade. At that time it was America who was buying from us and paying her balance in railway shares. But it soon became evident that many of the railways were not wanted and that the shares were nearly worthless. The dividends shrank away to nothing, and some of the companies became bankrupt. The same thing took place on a smaller scale in Russia, Austria, and other countries. Between 1865 and 1874 the railway mileage in Russia was multiplied nearly five-fold; in 1865 there were 2371 miles of railway, and in 1874 there were 11,556, showing an average railway construction of over 1000 miles a year sustained for nine years, which is a much more rapid development than was prudent for so poor a country as Russia. Of course at that time she was an excellent customer for our iron, and helped to swell our prosperity. It is evident that we may soon see a repetition of the same course of events. There is hardly a country in the world which is not at present contemplating additions to its railway system on a large scale. If only a small part of the schemes which are proposed for the next few years are carried out we shall certainly see a repetition of the inflation of 1872 and 1873, followed by a repetition of the depression which succeeded it. We may however hope that there will not again be so alarming a complication of diseases preying upon the social economy of the whole world. But at this moment the air is full of rumours of wars, and whether or not a great European war come to complete the parallel with the earliest year of the last decade, it is certain that the ever-increasing armaments of the continental nations are a most formidable impediment to healthy trade.

3. Immense sums were lavished in loans to foreign States. It seemed that no country could be too insignificant, or too unprincipled, or too insolvent to draw its millions from the pocket of the con-

fiding British investor. Lord Derby\* expressed his wonder that the King of Dahomey had never raised a loan, " but probably he was too much of a savage to see the advantage of being in debt." It has been estimated that† " English capitalists have lent more than three hundred millions sterling to States that will never pay them a shilling."

The results of this free-handed lending are at first very pleasant. It affords an outlet for capital and so helps to raise the rate of profit and interest in England; and at the same time, since we send out our loans, not in gold, but in ironclads and in railway bars, it stimulates the home manufactures. The creditors for a year or two are paid a high interest which all comes out of their own pockets. Soon there is a crash, and the payment of interest and the demand for railway bars cease simultaneously.‡ The following States are more or less defaulters; many of them have paid no dividend at all for several years :—Turkey, Egypt, Greece, Bolivia, Costa Rica, Ecuador, Honduras,

---

\* Speech at Rochdale, Jan. 2, 1879.
† Quoted by Lord Derby at Rochdale.
‡ We may cite the case of Paraguay as a typical instance of the process here described. In 1861 and 1872 she contracted two foreign loans of the nominal amount together of three millions at a rate of interest equivalent to ten per cent. Payment both of interest and of sinking fund ceased in 1874. "No part of the previous payments," according to the Report of the Select Parliamentary Committee on Foreign Loans, 1875, " was provided by the Government of Paraguay,

Mexico, Paraguay, Peru, St. Domingo, Uruguay, and Venezuela.

Of course these great loans helped to keep the balance of trade comparatively low, and " practical men" had the delight of seeing that we were sending our iron abroad, and getting nothing in return but the IOU of a bankrupt spendthrift!

4. The Suez Canal was opened on Nov. 17th, 1869, and about the same time the telegraph system of the world was becoming fairly complete. These undertakings, or at any rate the latter, helped directly to swell the inflation of our trade, but by far their most important effects were indirect. They revolutionized the commerce of the world, and caused it to be carried on in a very different manner from that of the old days. Now it is a race in which time is everything. It is said, for instance, that in a certain Exchange the desks nearest to the Telegraph Office fetch a much higher rent than those at a distance—such is the pecuniary value of a few yards start in a race thither.

Thus, there arose a demand for a new class of

---

but the whole was derived from the proceeds of the loans themselves."—"Statesman's Year Book," 1879.

Spain is an old defaulter: her debt, according to a certain high authority is divided into three classes. 1st, the active, which engages to pay interest now, and doesn't; 2nd, the deferred, which engages to pay interest at some future time (date unspecified), and won't; 3rd, the passive, which engages to pay interest neither now nor at any future time, and keeps its engagements strictly.

swift and powerful iron steam ships, which seemed to be rapidly superseding the sailing vessels in which our trade was formerly carried on. The change in this respect was very marked. In 1863, 574 steam vessels were employed in our foreign trade, with an aggregate tonnage of 371,201. The numbers and the tonnage have both been rapidly growing with hardly any break since that time; and in 1878 they stood at 1820 and 1,811,024 respectively. The fleet of sailing vessels could not in the nature of things decrease as rapidly as the steam ships could increase, but the diminution was very marked. The number of ships employed was at its maximum in 1853, when it stood at 8120; whilst at the end of 1878 it had diminished to 5235. The tonnage reached its maximum, *i.e.*, 3,646,150 in 1868; in 1874 it had fallen to 3,092,730, but since that year it has somewhat increased again.

One effect of this revolution in the course of trade was to give a great impetus to the trade in iron ships, and to others connected with it.

These seem to have been the chief primary causes that gave rise to the great inflation of trade which marked the earlier years of this decade in England; but we must not forget that secondary causes are excited by the primary, and are perhaps even stronger than those which gave them birth. In the most powerful modern electrical machines the current is at first generated by means of a piece of soft iron, which retains only faint traces of magnetism. But these traces are sufficient when the machine is set in motion by an engine to produce a slight current; this current itself makes the feeble magnet an electro-magnet, and the electro-magnetism reinforces the current. Thus current and magnet act and react on one another till both are of the utmost intensity. Just so is it with the causes of a commercial inflation; they act and react on one another till it has reached a pitch quite incommensurate with the original causes.

When any trade is in a state of abnormal activity, it seems to every one easy to make a fortune; prices are forced up, and there is a ready market for any quantity of produce. Every one is eager to extend his business. New mines are opened, new furnaces put in blast, new factories are built, new railways have to be made. In all these ways great quantities of wealth are spent in permanent works, and all the trades concerned are set in active motion, and in their turn communicate the excitement to yet others, or react on the first and increase their activity. Nor is this all; everybody seems to be better off than before; in some cases—that is to say, in the particular trades which are most inflated—they really are so. The result is a general spirit of reckless and extravagant expenditure on the part of all concerned, from capitalist to workman. The following description was written shortly after the inflation subsided:—"The rapid rise of prices and wages threw large systems of production entirely off their balance. More expenditure and less work took the place of frugality and diligence, and the acquisition of riches seemed to have become all at once so easy that the old virtues of diligence, skill, and patience could be laid aside both by men and masters." Thus the increased expenditure and inflated production spread itself more and more widely, and infected every industry.

Moreover, an inflation of legitimate trade such as we have described is generally accompanied by a horrible mushroom growth of a kind of trade, which at its best is gambling, and at its worst swindling. The commercial world is now so large, and the system of trading on credit so developed, that it was very easy to borrow money, and not always easy even for the honest and careful banker or bill-broker to distinguish between genuine and rotten bills. Hence there was a strong temptation to indulge in speculative ventures on the principle of "Heads, I win; tails, you lose," and much wild and unprofitable business was done. Some trading was not even intended to be profitable, but was directed solely to the floating of bills. One dealer is said to have made a habit of buying iron and selling again at 5s. a ton below cost price! This system was carried out on a gigantic scale by Messrs. Colley, who lived sumptuously for years upon borrowed money, and finally failed for several millions. Such dishonesty has been too often winked at by traders of repute who have found that dealing with reckless customers like these, if carried on with judgment, may be a profitable though dangerous method of gambling.

It is a lamentable feature in our economical system, that what we may call the natural relations of debtor and creditor are sometimes completely inverted, provided the debtor be bold enough, skilful enough, and deeply enough in debt. A debtor who owes a million can always extort more from his unfortunate creditors by the unanswerable threat of becoming bankrupt, and bringing hopeless ruin upon them. This was in brief the history of the City of Glasgow Bank, of the West of England Bank, and of many other failures.

Of course the rotten semblance of trade which was merely designed to forward " financial" operations added no less to the general excitement than did commerce of a more genuine character. The result was merely this, that we were enabled to live in great jubilation for a year or two upon our own capital, fancying all the while that we were rapidly becoming rich. In truth we were very rapidly becoming poor, as we may see from the dismal reaction which followed.

Hence we must not be surprised if we, who experienced a more marked inflation than our neighbours, should also have had a greater share of the reaction.

There are other reasons why we have lost more of our custom of late years than other countries. One is that we are a great manufacturing nation, and sell wares with which our neighbours if they are in poverty can dispense more easily than they can with the produce of agricultural countries. People restrict their consumption of ironclads and railway bars, or even of cotton, before they will go without bread.

Besides, the very extent of our trade makes us more liable than others to commercial misfortune; as M. Juglar remarks: "Les crises ne paraissent que chez les peuples dont le commerce est très développé. Là où il n'y a pas de division de travail, pas de commerce extérieur, le commerce intérieur est plus sûr." Our dealings with foreign nations are more extensive and more widely branching than those of any other country. Hence there is no one who suffers so much as we from disturbance or poverty in any part of the world.

The curious and interesting speculations which Professor Jevons has brought into prominence, as to the connection between commercial crises and sun spots, or rather the variation in the heating power of the sun of which sun spots are probably a symptom, seem to suggest that our general commercial prosperity is dependent to a degree hardly suspected before upon the well-being of India and China. However, the peculiarity of the present depression is that many causes all over the world have combined to anticipate and to drown the effects of famine in the East.

One very satisfactory reason why the exports of foreign nations have not fallen off as much as ours, is that they all have us for their best customer, and we, in spite of the general depression and impoverishment, have been able till lately to buy larger and larger quantities of their goods. The exports of France, for instance, to all countries except Great Britain had, in 1877, fallen off 17 per cent. from their value in 1873; but this was partly balanced by the fact that the exports to Great Britain had risen in value 15 per cent. in the same period. Of course no one reaped more advantage from the fact that the home market was not impoverished than our own traders and manufacturers. But this business did not swell the returns of foreign trade for us as it did for our neighbours. We shall see that this was a very substantial advantage to them from the subjoined table, which shows what percentage of the exports of each of the principal nations of the world comes to Great Britain :—

|  | Exports in Millions of £ | Percentage of Exports to Great Britain. |
|---|---|---|
| Russia in Europe, 1877 | 80½ | 29·2 |
| Sweden, 1877 | 12 | 54·1 |
| Holland, 1877 | 44 | 24·8 |
| Belgium, 1878 | 44½ | 22·4 |
| France, 1878 | 127 | 28·7 |
| Spain, 1875 | 18 | 34·9 |
| Italy, 1878 | 35 | 9·7 |
| United States, 1878 | 141¾ | 57·7 |
| China, 1878 |  | 42·6 |

Unfortunately, the values of the German exports are not given. The percentages are reckoned on the exports of home produce wherever these are given separately, for the latest year which is included in the Statistical Abstract.

There has, no doubt, been a considerable development of industry in several foreign countries, especially America, Germany, France and Belgium, which has caused these countries to be worse customers of ours than they used to be. This is very unpleasant for us; but we have no right to complain. They are following at a great distance in our footsteps, imitating the vast development to which we attained years ago, when we became the clothiers and iron workers of the whole world. We certainly have no inalienable right to that position. We can only keep it by the qualities which won it for us, by indefatigable hard work, by skill, perseverance, and above all by good faith and harmonious working of masters and men.

All these qualities are being undermined by the spirit of trades-unionism — which is a spirit of short-sighted selfishness.

I intend no offence to trades-unions; the spirit which I have ventured to call trades-unionism is not an essential of the trades-union. Trades-unions there may be and there are, which are conducted in a thoroughly enlightened spirit, and which the masters find a most useful instrument in dealing with the mass of the workmen.

But too often their principles have been opposed to the true manufacturing interest of the country. They have acted as though the masters and men had no interests in common, but were natural enemies. Work is simply a contrivance for getting wages out of the master without any care either for its quantity or its quality. They have not perceived that there *is* a wage fund, other than that fancied by political economists; that this wage fund is simply the things produced, and that it is the interest of master and man alike to make this dividend as large as they can. When they have done this they will have to decide somehow, by fighting if they will, how it is to be divided. The good workman, the workman who made England what it is, took a pride in good work and in hard work. The modern workman, dominated by the fear of his fellows, will not venture to put his heart into his work. It is not etiquette to do more than one is obliged.

Nor is the spirit of trades-unionism—of eye work—confined to the men. It has infected the masters also. We often hear of the decline of English goods. It is probably not in any one industry that the quality of our goods is falling off; Sheffield steel, for instance, has not the same unsullied fame that it once had. There are such things now as Sheffield razors made to sell and not to cut. But the most conspicuous example of worthless and adulterated manufacture on a large scale is to be found in our cotton goods. With regard to some of these Mrs. Siddons might well have asked her famous question, "BUT WILL THEY WASH?" in her most deeply tragic tones. In more senses than one they will not wash. We cannot expect that foreign nations will long consent to buy from us cotton which has more size than cotton in it.

Before quitting this subject we may quote som

weighty sentences which occur in a sermon preached by the Bishop of Manchester. The warning contained in them comes with special force and appropriateness from the Bishop of that city which is the great centre of the cotton trade, and one of the greatest sinners against the laws of commercial morality. He said,[*] "I do not dream foolish dreams, but I feel that unless there is a radical change in our lives, in our motives, and in our conduct one towards another, the prosperity of this country is doomed. If we are perpetually to have strikes between capital and labour; if we are to trade as we have for ten or twelve years been trading upon fictitious capital; and if the whole surface of society is to be undermined with rottenness and trickery, so that men hardly know whom to trust—if this is to be the normal condition of our lives, I do not see how society is to go on. It was once a great puzzle—I will not say to a great statesman, but to a great Englishman—how her Majesty's Government was to be carried on, but it is a much more important question how society is to go on in the present condition of things."

Our commerce is no doubt largely injured by protective tariffs. Our manufactures are handi-

---

[*] Sermon preached in the Chapel of the Blind Asylum, Old Trafford, Jan. 5, 1879.

capped in almost every country in the world by the heavy duties which they have to pay.

More than thirty per cent. of the whole falling off of our exports in 1878 as compared with 1873 was due to the decrease of our exports to America, which fell to less than half their former value. Now, the greater part of this diminution was, as we have already stated, due to the intense depression which has prevailed in that country, but it was also largely caused by the exorbitant protective duties levied. Indeed, it is a remarkable illustration of the evil effects of protection, that it should so greatly raise the cost of production in America, that we are able at all to compete with her manufacturers in their own markets, and that our exports thither have not been annihilated by the tariff against which they have to contend.

We are more or less hampered by protection in our access to almost all the markets of the world, except those of most of our own dependencies; for though there is no other tariff so extravagantly prohibitive as that of the United States, there is hardly any foreign country which does not exact duties that seriously interfere with our trade. One or two even of our own colonies have introduced a rigorous system of protection.

The greatest injury, however, that protection inflicts upon us is indirect. The nations which maintain it greatly impoverish themselves, and thus make themselves worse customers than they would otherwise be for our produce. If America inflicts loss upon herself we must bear part of the burden.

We may, however, console ourselves by the thought that although the American tariff causes great loss to us indirectly as well as directly, yet at the same time it materially helps us by paralysing her in her capacity of rival in third markets. It is true that the American exports of manufactured goods have been growing somewhat, but we have seen that this is an unhealthy and unprofitable trade. The quantity of cotton goods produced under the stimulating influence of protection had completely outstripped the requirements of the home market, and consequently it had to be "slaughtered" abroad—that is to say, disposed of at ruinously low prices. Any remunerative competition on the part of American manufacturers in third markets is an impossibility under their present commercial policy. The same thing holds good in a less degree of other countries which have more moderate tariffs. Probably one reason why we have retained so much of our manufacturing pre-eminence is that other nations have chosen thus to weight themselves in the struggle for third markets. Hence we need not be too much disheartened by this perverse policy. We cannot say whether any particular tariff does us most harm or good, but in every case it is sure to be helping us in one market while it harms us in another. Provided only we do our part strenuously, we may trust that no foreign nation can fatally injure us either by protection or by free trade.

There is another cause to which too much importance has often been ascribed by partisan speakers and writers, but which no doubt contributed somewhat to retard and smother any tendency which there might be to returning prosperity in trade. For several years there were perpetually most serious apprehensions of a great European war. It was believed by many that this uncertainty was the principal cause of the protracted depression of trade, and that if security could only be restored to us trade would speedily revive. When the Treaty of Berlin was signed, all immediate fear of an European war passed away for a time, but trade did not revive. On the contrary, the depression only reached its culminating point in the summer of 1879. It is true that the political horizon did not become completely clear, that a cloud appeared in Afghanistan which quickly grew to very serious proportions, and that we have been engaged in two petty wars, if, indeed, we ought to call wars petty which so seriously strained our resources as these have done. However, it would be absurd to ascribe great influence to political troubles such as these when the Treaty of Berlin did so little to relieve trade. The truth is that the real causes of our distress are deeper and more widespread than anything of this kind. Our traders would be active enough we may be sure if they saw any good chance of making profits. It is not so much sound trade as rash speculation which is checked by political distrust. In this I refer to the direct results of political uncertainty, not to those of increased taxation, which no doubt has done us serious injury.

The real and deep-seated cause of all our distress is this, the whole world has been consuming more than it has produced, and is consequently in a state of impoverishment and cannot buy our wares. It inevitably feels the pinch of that fundamental law of political economy, "You can't eat your cake and have it."

We have already touched on the principal cause of English impoverishment, it is to be sought for in the over-expenditure of the time of inflation. If the wealth which was spent in the production of manufacturing instruments which were not needed had been thrown into the sea, it would hardly have been more completely wasted. At least, in that case, we should have been saved the grinding misery of over-production. By over-production we do not mean absolute over-production. Such a thing as that is hardly possible in this world. We mean over-production of particular goods.

We cannot feed upon iron bars, or clothe ourselves with them; hence, if we are producing more of these than we can exchange for corn and wool, and the like, there is certainly over-production of iron bars; but absolute over-production there cannot be while the community has yet many wants unsatisfied.

The spirit of reckless and speculative outlay upon the instruments of production which would not yield remunerative returns, together with the excessive personal expenditure which it engendered, did more than anything else, or at any rate more than any act of our own, to undermine our prosperity.

A large part of this expenditure was not merely wasted, but was worse than wasted. Much of that which the nation spends upon drink is not merely a vast direct drain upon its resources, but also does mischief economical as well as moral which is in amount incalculable, by sapping energy and self-respect, by stimulating crime and pauperism.

Another deplorable feature of our social system is to be seen in the strikes, of which there have been so many unfortunate examples of late years. It is hard to form an adequate conception of the waste and loss which these have brought upon us.

Strikes are the natural concomitant of a decline in trade or even of a mere fall in prices. It is natural that the labourers should resist the reduction of wages which these render inevitable, with greater strenuousness than they will demand an advance when it is their just due. Strikes impoverish the country not only by the suspension of the branches of trade immediately involved, but also in many cases by disorganising and paralysing other branches of industry.

The direct loss to both masters and men is very great; the masters have many fixed expenses, such as rent, interest, taxes, depreciation of machinery, and the like, which they must meet as much in times of idleness as in full work. Their trade must, indeed, be bad if they do not lose by a strike.

To the men loss and suffering are still more inevitable. Whilst the strike continues they are earning nothing; and it seldom happens that they gain their object; still more seldom is the gain worth the price at which it has been bought.

The reason of this is simple. The masters will not in most cases incur the risk of a strike except under a strong necessity. They will make any possible concession sooner than submit to the total loss of earnings which it implies. It may, indeed, under special circumstances be convenient to them, but this is highly exceptional. Hence, as the masters have so little choice in the matter, the workmen are almost sure to be beaten. Yet it does not follow that a strike should never be resorted to; only that more moderation and judgment should be shown. There is a real and important opposition of interest between employer and man, in spite of all that the political economists tell us about the "wages fund." There *is* such a fund—that is to say, the things produced—which must be divided between master and man; and assuredly neither party will get as much as they ought—that is to say, as much as they can—unless they are prepared to back up their claim if necessary by war. If the fear of strikes is to be efficacious it must be real. It is visionary to suppose that employers would give as high wages as can be exacted by the fear of a strike, if that fear were to be removed. They will care little for a threat of "mantraps and spring guns," unless the traps are set and the guns loaded.

Strikes, like war or capital punishment, ought to

be preventive, and succeed only when they are not called into play.  When they are resorted to, they have *ipso facto* failed.  Thus, it is their real efficacy which causes their apparent futility.  The fear of a strike prevents any employer from reducing wages unless he is compelled to do so; and then, strong in the strength of the tutelary goddesses of the Andrians,\* he is sure to win.

Certainly, arbitration is the more excellent way in trade disputes no less than in those of nations, and in both arbitration has done great things, which we may trust are earnest of yet greater.  Thanks to arbitration the coal fields and the iron works of the north have till lately enjoyed peace through a time of wearing depression, and in spite of many reductions of wages.

But in truth, though arbitration may do much to avert wars and strikes, it is hard to see how it can ever completely supersede either the one or the other.  Unless the opposing parties are coerced by some higher power, an appeal to force must always be open to them, and it is hardly probable so long as human nature remains what it is that these wretched expedients will ever become wholly obsolete.

In a trade dispute the forces in action are, on

---

\* " Poverty and Helplessness," *vide* Herodotus. vii. 111.

the one side, the power to refuse to work, and on the other, to refuse to employ. The rate of wages must be fixed at a point of equilibrium where the men are willing to work and the masters to employ. Arbitration cannot supersede those forces, or introduce some new principle by which wages are to be adjusted. Its function is merely to discover this point of equilibrium peaceably and economically; but the forces remain dormant, not inoperative.

We have already spoken of the ruinous foreign loans to insolvent States which have so grievously impoverished this country, to the extent it is said of 300 millions, and also of the disastrous series of bad harvests which have marked the last five years, the loss on which is reckoned at over 20 millions annually. These two causes must have done much to undermine the wealth of the country.

Another cause of impoverishment to England, less serious, than any we have yet mentioned, but still considerable, is to be found in the rapid increase of public expenditure and taxation which has, by an unfortunate accident, precisely coincided with the period of depression. During the ten years from 1864 to 1873 inclusive, the average annual expenditure was £69,304,063.*

---

\* The increase of expenditure is not to be regarded as a real net increase; it is to some extent capable of satisfactory explanation. But as our present intention is neither to attack nor to defend the Govern-

This includes several extraordinary expenses—viz., £5,600,000 for the Abyssinian expedition, £760,000 for the New Zealand war, and £1,460,000 on account of the Franco-German war. We may therefore fairly take the expenditure of the ten previous years as our basis in reckoning the increased expenditure to which we have been subject during the depression of trade.

Now, the aggregate public expenditure during the seven years from 1874 to 1880 has been £557,568,834, giving a yearly average of £79,652,690. The increase of average annual expenditure is £10,348,684, and the increase in the aggregate expenditure for the seven years over the due amount for seven years as deduced from the average of the ten previous years is £72,440,791.

The Chancellor of the Exchequer is by no means to be envied the task on which he is at present engaged, of providing for the heavy deficit which will be produced by the combined effect of war expenditure in two continents and a revenue which was originally calculated in a spirit at once too san-

---

ment, but simply to call attention to one among many causes of impoverishment to the country, we have not thought it necessary to enter into these points, but have given the amount of the "total gross expenditure," just as it is set down in the Official Statistical Abstract. I have chosen the years beginning with 1873-74 for my starting-point, because in that year (which almost entirely fell under the administration of the late Government) the marked increase began.

F

guine and too timid, and which has of late shown an unaccountable and disconcerting shrinkage.

There can be no doubt that the taxation of this country is a heavy burden on its trade and industry, and that the increased expenditure has sensibly added to this burden; but I do not believe either that the late depression of trade was mainly caused by impoverishment at home or that the increased taxation had so large a share as other causes in producing that impoverishment.

It must be allowed that the Government themselves seem to lay more stress upon this cause than I have done, since they declined to raise any of the taxes for the past financial year in order to meet their deficit. The Chancellor of the Exchequer in his Budget speech said: "The present is not the time in which additional taxation would be borne without considerable distress. Now, considerable distress does not mean merely a great amount of complaint and grumbling; but it means a diminution of spending power, which diminution of spending power necessarily affects the trading community and the agricultural community, and tends to keep down the condition of the country, which we rather hope to be advancing and improving. For my own part I may say that unless under a sense of necessity and absolute duty, I should look with very great reluctance upon any proposal to make a large addition to our taxation."

The approaching Budget will be a severe test of the courage and honesty of the Government. They will have to face a heavy deficit on the past year which ought to be provided for by a considerable increase of taxation; but it will be a wonderful feat if they adequately reform their habit of shifty finance on the very eve of a General Election.

# CHAPTER IV.

## THE CAUSES WHICH GAVE RISE TO THE DEPRESSION.
### 2. ABROAD.

IF we take a rapid survey of the various nations of the world, we shall find that the same cause has been at work among almost all of them in many different shapes; they have been consuming too much and producing too little, and have consequently come to a condition of poverty and have nothing to spend on our wares.

Before considering the countries separately it will be interesting to give some indication of the degree in which each has contributed to the decrease of our trade.

The following tables show the extent to which our exports of home produce to each of the principal countries of the world had fallen off in 1878 as compared with 1873, and also the percentage which each country contributed towards the total falling off in that period which amounted to £62,315,689.

## Foreign Countries.

| | Exports of British and Irish produce in 1873. (000 omitted.) | Exports of British and Irish produce in 1878. (000 omitted.) | Decrease or Increase. (000 omitted.) | Decrease or Increase per cent. | Percentage of Decrease or Increase on the total Decrease. |
|---|---|---|---|---|---|
| Russia | 8,998 | 6,559 | −2,438 | −27·3 | −3·9 |
| Sweden and Norway | 5,031 | 2,798 | −2,232 | −44·3 | −3·6 |
| Denmark, Iceland and Danish West Indies | 3,023 | 1,764 | −1,258 | −41·6 | −2 |
| Germany | 27,270 | 19,457 | −7,813 | −28·6 | −12·5 |
| Holland | 16,745 | 9,303 | −7,442 | −44·4 | −11·9 |
| Java, &c. | 760 | 1,662 | +902 | +118·6 | +1·4 |
| Belgium | 7,201 | 5,525 | −1,675 | −23·2 | −2·7 |
| France | 17,292 | 14,825 | −2,467 | −14·2 | −4 |
| Portugal | 2,934 | 2,116 | −818 | −27·8 | −1·3 |
| Spain | 3,736 | 3,211 | −525 | −14 | −0·8 |
| Italy | 7,444 | 5,364 | −2,080 | −27·9 | −3·3 |
| Austrian Territories | 1,484 | 763 | −721 | −48·6 | −1·2 |
| Turkey | 7,733 | 7,748 | +14 | +0·2 | +0·02 |
| Egypt | 6,222 | 2,194 | −4,029 | −64·7 | −6·5 |
| United States | 33,574 | 14,552 | −19,022 | −56·6 | −30·5 |
| Mexico | 1,194 | 773 | −421 | −35·1 | −0·7 |
| Central America, Haiti & San Domingo, New Granada, Venezuela, Ecuador | 4,583 | 2,770 | −1,812 | −39·5 | −2·9 |
| Brazil | 7,544 | 5,578 | −1,966 | −26 | −3·1 |
| Uruguay, Argentine Republic | 5,491 | 3,315 | −2,175 | −39·6 | −3·5 |
| Chili | 3,165 | 1,191 | −1,974 | −62·3 | −3·1 |
| Peru | 2,524 | 1,369 | −1,154 | −45·7 | −1·8 |
| China | 4,882 | 3,738 | −1,144 | −23·4 | −1·8 |
| Japan | 1,680 | 2,615 | +935 | +55·7 | +1·5 |
| Other foreign countries | 8,519 | 7,415 | −1,104 | −12·9 | −1·8 |
| Total, foreign countries | 188,836 | 126,611 | −62,224 | −32·9 | −99·85 |

## British Possessions.

| | Exports of British and Irish Produce in 1873. (000 omitted.) | Exports of British and Irish Produce in 1878. (000 omitted.) | Decrease or Increase. (000 omitted.) | Decrease or Increase per cent. | Percentage of Decrease or Increase on the total Decrease. |
|---|---|---|---|---|---|
| Canada and Newfoundland | 8,619 | 6,436 | − 2,183 | − 25·3 | − 3·5 |
| West India Islands, British Guiana, British Honduras | 3,481 | 2,760 | − 721 | − 20·7 | − 1·1 |
| Australia and New Zealand | 17,610 | 19,573 | + 1,963 | + 10 | + 3·1 |
| British India, Ceylon | 22,406 | 24,080 | + 1,674 | + 7·4 | + 2·7 |
| Straits Settlements, Hong Kong | 5,517 | 4,646 | − 870 | − 15·7 | − 1·4 |
| British Possessions in Africa | 5,037 | 5,785 | + 748 | + 14·8 | + 1·2 |
| Other Possessions | 3,656 | 2,954 | − 702 | − 19·2 | − 1·1 |
| Total to British Possessions | 66,328 | 66,237 | − 91 | − 0·14 | − 0·15 |

These tables present a lively and dismal picture of almost universal destitution among our foreign customers. It is, however, cheering to observe that some of our own possessions are amongst the isolated exceptions in the general gloom, and that on the whole our exports to them have hardly fallen off at all.

The main cause which has led to the impoverishment of the nations of Europe has been war and the preparation for war. The total cost to France of the war and foreign occupation of 1870-1873 are reckoned at £371,515,280. This includes the indemnity of £200,000,000 to Germany, and may therefore be regarded as a statement of the total war expenses on both sides. But these figures, large as they are, do not express a tithe of the real price that France and other nations have had to pay for war; they merely represent the disbursements from the National treasuries for the expenses of one actual war. They tell us nothing of the waste involved to the country by the employment of great bodies of men on unproductive work; they tell us nothing of the effect upon the industry of the country of taking away its young men in the prime of their youth, and forcing them to spend several years in learning military exercises instead of preparing themselves for their work in life. Nor do these figures tell us of the perpetual and almost unendurable pecuniary burden of the peace establishments.

For though a modern war is a terrible calamity, which causes a horrible drain of lives as well as of wealth to the conquerors not less than to the conquered, yet it seldom lasts long, and consequently does not inflict such deep injuries upon a country as the unceasing burden of maintaining a whole nation in arms.

The numbers of the armies maintained in time of peace by the four great continental powers exceed two millions. But the number of the men who have passed through war training, and who might be called upon to serve in time of war, is probably three times as great.

It is not to be wondered at that nations with such a terrible canker as this, eating away their prosperity, should be poor customers for our goods. In our table, although Russia shows a great decrease, Turkey shows a slight improvement; but the first effect of the deadly war in which they were engaged was to paralyse the purchasing powers of both.

We have already spoken of the evil effects at home of over expenditure upon permanent instruments of production. We may see the same thing in a more marked shape in Germany as well as in Austria and America. The manufactures of Germany were largely and unhealthily stimulated by the great influx of French gold, and an inflation was produced similar in its nature and its results to that in England. Perhaps the main difference was that it was less profitable though not less excessive than the English inflation. Hence the collapse was all the severer. The following description given by Mr. Brassey* of the state of things in Germany is well worth quotation:—

"Every description of industrial enterprise was

---

\* *Nineteenth Century*, May, 1879.

undertaken with rash precipitation, and on a vast scale. The agricultural population gathered into the great cities, causing a portentous rise in rents and in the cost of living. The working classes were dazzled by the sudden rise of wages; they lost their self-control, and became self-indulgent and extravagant. The landed and middle classes suffered from the general increase of prices and the cost of living, and they too sought for compensation in wild and disastrous speculation. The effects of the commercial mania which followed upon the military triumphs in France have not yet disappeared."

The magnitude of the German export trade is neither a sign nor a cause of national prosperity; it is simply a sign of the stagnation and poverty of the home market which, combined with the too rapid development of the means of production, caused a great and unprofitable overflow abroad. Another witness writes of recent German trade, that " it is of a very fitful, disorganised, and altogether muddled kind, owing to the burst of insanity which came over the German race after its successes in the war with France."

Precisely the same remarks apply to the case of America, where the expansion of exports and the contraction of imports alike are in great measure due to the poverty and inelasticity of the home market. One natural effect of protection under the influence of the great speculative inflation, was to cause an excessive construction of mills and furnaces. When the home demand fell off, goods had to be sent abroad and got rid of at any sacrifice.

We have already mentioned the extravagant railway expenditure which has been so harmful to Russia and Austria.

The various small States of Europe—Belgium, Holland, Denmark, Norway, Sweden, Greece—have not themselves had any special cause of impoverishment; but they have suffered deeply from the general collapse of trade, as we may plainly see by reference to the table on p. 69.

We have not unnaturally heard much lately of Belgian competition, for the Belgians have certainly succeeded to some extent in entering into successful competition with our manufacturers on their own soil. We hear of Belgian iron used in the very centre of the English and Scotch iron-fields, whilst our glass makers have been thrown into despair by the sale of Belgian glass at prices which they are quite unable to rival. With regard to their competition in iron, our iron-masters may take some comfort from the small volume of Belgian iron which is imported into England and other countries, when compared with that which we produce. The damage done to our manufacturers by competition on so small a scale can not have been great.*

With regard to glass, Belgian competition seems to be more serious. We are being fairly beaten by them in the production of cheap glass. The total exports of glass from Belgium in 1878 were valued at £1,582,520 of which £1,163,917 were brought to Great Britian. The exports of British glass in the same year were only valued at £755,884. This successful competition in the manufacture of glass appears to arise partly from a superiority of manual dexterity and care on the part of Belgian workmen and manufacturers, partly from the absence of certain harassing trades-union rules. It is not, however, a remunerative business; excessive competition among Belgian glass works has forced down prices to a rate which leaves no margin for profits, and thus for the present they can undersell us in our own markets. Such at least is the account brought back by certain members of a leading English firm of glass makers, who were lately sent to Belgium to examine the state of glass making there.

If we look further East we find the most grievous poverty arising from gross misgovernment as well

---

* The total exports of iron from Belgium in 1878 were 193,000 tons. Her exports to England in the same year were 65,122 tons. The quantity of British iron exported in 1878 was 2,296,860, and the total quantity of pig-iron produced in that year was 6,381,051 tons.

as from natural causes. We need say little of Turkey; she has been ruined by misgovernment, and now the war has reduced her to such a hopeless state of bankruptcy that it would be impossible for her to introduce effectual reforms if she would.

The same remark applies to Egypt, which is in an impoverished state through the extravagant expenditure and the cruel misgovernment and rapacity of the late Khedive. Such a country as this has no great resources for trade when it has exhausted the credulity of foreign investors. Hence our exports to Egypt have fallen off by more than half since 1873.

India was one of the very few countries which received more of our goods in 1877 and 1878 than in 1873. But there can be no doubt that India is in a dreadful state of poverty and over-taxation. We maintain there an expensive Army and Civil Service which, whether it be superfluous or not, is certainly beyond the power of the people to sustain without grinding over-taxation, and without the help of one most iniquitous but most profitable monopoly.* It is probable that the growth of our exports to India is in some degree accounted for by

---

\* The gross revenue derived from opium averaged during the ten years, 1869 to 1878, more than 8¼ millions sterling.

the recent construction of great lines of railway which have developed her internal commerce, opening out new markets for our cotton goods. However, when we take into account the poverty of the country and the notoriously unprofitable condition of the trade with it, we shall see reason to suspect that the development is for the most part not of this healthy kind, but like the development of the imports from the United States and Germany, the overflow of a glutted market, which must be relieved somewhere at any sacrifice.

Our exports to China in 1878 show a considerable diminution, which was mainly owing to the famine. These famines or scarcities having recurred decennially with great regularity are, as I have already pointed out (on page 51), regarded by Mr. Jevons as the actuating cause of our regular decennial crises. *Now*, at any rate, they have only contributed their share to aggravate and prolong mischief already done by many other causes.

The various South American and Central American States show a considerable decrease of trade. Here the cause is mainly one which we have already touched upon. Their former imports were in great measure bought with borrowed money; now their credit is gone, and they have ceased to be our customers. Nor is this a trade the loss of which we need greatly regret, although the falling off is very large in amount.

We have already mentioned the principal causes which impoverished the United States, and caused the decrease of her imports both from Britain and from the rest of the world, so they need not be dwelt upon here. They were mainly extravagant railway expenditure, encouraged as we have seen by unwise legislation, and an excessive and wasteful expenditure on manufactures, which was artificially stimulated by protection.

We see throughout the world one great cause leading to the ruin of trade. Everywhere men have been consuming more than they had to consume—that is to say, more than they have produced; in some cases because they have produced too little, in others because they have consumed too much.

There has been another class of causes at work to which we can only assign second-rate importance, but which has undoubtedly injured commerce to a considerable extent, by turning it into gambling, and by aggravating the financial difficulties of particular countries.

There have been serious derangements of the currency in many countries. America, till last year, had an inconvertible paper currency; Russia and Turkey have still a great excess of depreciated notes. The inconvenience which this brings upon commerce can hardly be exaggerated. The fluctuations in value of an inconvertible paper currency are violent and impossible to foresee. Hence trade is carried on at a great disadvantage. Merchants do not care for transactions in which by some sudden movement of the rate of exchange a profit may be unexpectedly converted into a heavy loss, and in which really sound trade is an impossibility.

This excessive issue of paper money is merely the device of an impecunious government for forcibly exacting a contribution from all creditors among its subjects. It introduces disorganization and confusion into all money dealings to a degree quite out of proportion with the ill-gotten gains which are reaped from the measure.

Another cause of distress which has affected many countries of the world is similar to this, but even more serious; the depreciation of silver. For some years silver has been very much below its old value in relation to gold. Its present market price is 52*d.*, which, although somewhat higher than the lowest point it reached, is still much below its old price of 60*d.*

The main causes of this depreciation seem to have been the discovery of the immensely productive mines of Nevada, coupled with the demonetisation of silver by Germany, and the restriction of its coinage by the Latin Union, a restriction which is practically equivalent to its disuse. All the richer nations of the world now use the gold standard, and exact their debts in that metal.

Thus, the loss by exchange is a heavy burden upon the finances of silver-using countries, such as India, which have to make large foreign payments.

Then the injury which the fluctuation in value of silver does to the trade of these countries is immense. It has all the effects of an inconvertible paper currency in turning honest trade into speculative gambling. Those who are most experienced in Indian commerce will confess most readily their inability to foretell the value of the rupee. Indeed, the matter is so complicated that I have heard a broker of fifteen years' experience in the East, express his belief that the exchanges do not depend on any principle at all except the whim of the bankers!

Except with respect to old contracts it is the fluctuation, not the permanent depreciation of a currency which harms a country, or the traders who have dealings with it. Money is merely an instrument of exchange and a measure of value; the one essential point is that it should be steady. Prices adjust themselves in the long run to any permanent change (though friction sometimes makes the process very slow), but they cannot adjust themselves to a currency which incessantly varies by leaps and bounds.

## CHAPTER V.

### REMEDIES PROPOSED FOR THE DEPRESSION.

I HAVE now completed my sketch of the principal causes both at home and abroad which have led to our distress, though my account professes to be nothing more— especially in the case of foreign countries—than the barest outline. We are now in a position to consider a few of the principal remedies which were proposed for the distress under which we were labouring.

We shall find plenty of these ready to our hand, but we shall find that in too many instances they are either out of our power to apply, or else if applied would be futile.

In the first place we have from Lord Beaconsfield a piece of advice which, although, when it was delivered, it sounded to many almost like bitter mockery—yet undoubtedly it was the true and wise solution to the difficulty. He told us that we must rely upon the " alchemy of patience," which would certainly bring a remedy in time. His words have proved true. It was only time and patience which have been able to bring about a real amelioration of the state of trade in this country, and in the whole world. During the weary years of waiting, although profits have everywhere seemed so low, yet really the whole world has been consuming less than it has produced, and so has gradually recovered from its impoverishment, and prepared itself for the new burst of railway making, inflated trade, and inflated expenditure which is now coming upon us. This process of enforced economy is a far more powerful remedy than any which we or any other nation can deliberately apply.

We have seen that the main causes of the depression of trade are to be sought for abroad, and we can do but little to relieve the foreign distress which reacts so disastrously upon ourselves. It is true that we have ascribed much influence to economical and social faults at home. But the remedy for these is in most cases moral, and under the control of individuals, not of the nation.

For instance, it would do much towards the cure of our distress if we became more honest in our work and in our business habits. If our financiers and merchants would give up practices which are at best gambling, and at worst robbery; if our manufacturers would do their best to make their goods *good*, and would not care so exclusively for cheapness, without regard to quality; if our workmen would do more genuine work, and give their first thought to doing their work well, and their second to getting well paid for it, instead of thinking only of the wages, and caring nothing for the quality of the work—in a word, if the world would become honest, we should soon tide over our difficulties. Now all this, unfortunately, sounds like a somewhat Utopian sermon delivered *urbi et orbi*. The question how the city and the world are to be induced to obey it is hopelessly bewildering. Legislation may do something. By improving the bankruptcy laws it may perhaps make the game of "Heads, I win, tails, you lose," somewhat more difficult and dangerous to play. At present it would seem that no one can get more comfortable or pleasant treatment than a fraudulent bankrupt, provided only his deficit is on a large enough scale. If a man steal several millions of pounds, thereby ruining thousands of innocent people, he will probably escape with little or no punishment.

Moreover, legislation has done something and may perhaps do more to check dishonest and adulterated work; but it can do very little; nor can it do anything to make the work of workmen more genuine and hearty.

Again, it would do perhaps more than anything else to relieve the national distress, and in every respect, moral as well as physical and economical, to raise the condition of the people if we could abolish or alleviate that great national curse, drunkenness, which more than anything else eats away the wealth, the strength, and the moral character of the nation.

A suggestion made by Mr. Forster deserves careful consideration. It seems to be thought by many that we have reduced our hours of labour beyond what is needful. They are shorter than those which some other nations find compatible with health and strength. The Belgians, in particular, work for hours which an English workman would reckon impossible. It is obvious that if we shorten our time of work unnecessarily, we are heavily handicapping ourselves in the struggle with other nations for manufacturing supremacy.

But we must remember that the amount of goods produced, or of wages earned, is not the sole test of the proper hours of labour, but the real happiness and comfort of the labourer.

If the hours are unduly lengthened he sacrifices to his work everything that makes life worth having. "A land overcrowded with a dense mass of ill-fed, ill-clothed, and poorly-housed inhabitants is surely a miserable spectacle. Modern Europe, alas! contains populations in whom it might almost seem that the Mosaic prediction had been fulfilled. 'In the morning thou shalt say would God it were even, and at even thou shalt say would God it were morning.'"*

On the other hand, if the hours are too short, we shall inevitably lose our foreign custom, and the cotton spinners must starve. In view of this dilemma, Mr. Forster well suggested that the proper hours of labour should be determined by a mixed body of masters and men.

In contrast with this demand for longer hours and harder work, we may consider a contrary idea, which has found much favour in some quarters, that all our distress sprang from over-production, and that the true remedy was restriction of output. We were told that if all our mills and furnaces worked half-time the painful glut of the market would come to an end, and there would be a return of remunerative prices.

It is true that our trouble sprang in a great degree from over-production; but it does not necessarily follow that restricted work was the proper cure. In the first place, the over-production was mainly a thing of the past, whose evil effects would have been aggravated, not alleviated by restriction. That wealth which we wasted on an excessive stock of the instruments of production is lost and gone; nothing can repair the injury done

---

* Mr. Brassey in the *Nineteenth Century*, May, 1879.

then, unless we can find a market for all that these instruments can produce. Now this we assuredly could not do by restricting the hours of work. If we did so we should enhance the cost of production to ourselves; but we have too many and too keen competitors abroad, who are themselves suffering from a glut as severe as ours, for us to expect that an enhancement of cost and a diminution of production in England would sensibly raise prices throughout the world. It would merely give our foreign rivals the opportunity for which they long, of stepping into our place.

We could not, indeed, go on producing more cotton goods and yarn than our neighbours would buy from us; but the cure had to be found, not in working short time, which the masters felt instinctively was an impossible solution of the problem, but on the contrary in careful economy and contrivance, as well as in a process of weeding out the least efficient and poorest mills, by a kind of natural selection of the fittest and by the failure of the least fit. This process was very bitter, but it was the only remedy, or the least ruinous remedy, for economical faults committed long ago.

We have already touched upon the question of strikes. Certainly the abolition of strikes, whether by means of arbitration or in any other way, would be a reform of the highest value, both socially and economically. It is a reform which has already in great measure been carried out, and which has been very beneficial in its effects. But it is not easy to believe that strikes will ever become wholly obsolete. We shall probably always be liable to occasional outbursts of temper or unreason, which no arbitrator can appease.

We see that the time of a first revival of trade is marked by many strikes as well as the period of sinking trade. It is natural that when workmen's wages are at the lowest ebb they should be impatient—no doubt sometimes too impatient—to reap advantage from the first improvement.

Emigration will do much for us, not, indeed, by clearing away our surplus population. Malthus showed long ago that it could do little in that respect, and no doubt he was right, except in peculiar cases, such as that of Ireland after the potato famine.

As a rule it is those who go that reap the benefit, whilst the pressure on those who remain behind is not materially lessened, because the power of population to increase is sufficient to fill up all ordinary gaps. At the same time emigration will do much to help the prosperity of the old country by opening out great continents to be our markets. There is a boundless field still left for British enterprise in the wilds of Australia and Africa.

Agriculture as we saw is very depressed in this country, and though this depression is in part due to temporary causes, especially to an extraordinary succession of bad harvests, it is also probably in some measure permanent.

Ricardo pointed out that the rent of any particular land is regulated by the difference between its net produce and that of the worst land which it would be worth while to cultivate at all.

Although this theory is liable to misapprehension, and has been attacked by an eminent modern economist, yet undoubtedly it is true in theory; that is to say, true under the hypothesis—so familiar to physicists—of a world without friction; whilst in practice it is a rough approximation to the truth.

We must understand, of course, that the theory does not imply that the land "on the margin of cultivation" is a sort of standard to which landlord and tenant refer with unanimous reverence when haggling over the question of rent; but that rents will of their own accord, by virtue of the ordinary laws of supply and demand, conform themselves with a certain measure of accuracy to the value which the theory assigns for them.

It is perhaps hardly necessary to add that when we speak of the rent of land being regulated by its "fertility," the word fertility is to be understood in its widest sense, as including not only what is ordinarily called fertility, but every other element which contributes to the total profits which the land brings in to the farmer. Of these elements one of the most important is the distance from the market.

America has been practically brought nearer to us by her railways and by the cheapening of steam navigation as well as by improvements in the methods of carrying meat. Indeed, it would seem that within the last few months Australia has been brought within the circle of countries competing to supply the English meat market. Thus the margin between the better land and the worst that can profitably supply our markets has been reduced. If this be so the necessary remedy is evident. Farming having become unprofitable, rents must and will fall. The wisest landlord will be the first to recognise this and to avoid the loss of tenantless farms.

We have seen the incalculable mischief that is inflicted on us and on all the world by war and the preparation for war. Far the greater part of the money raised by taxation throughout the world is spent either in providing for future wars or in paying for those that are past.

*We* cannot do much towards getting rid of this terrible incubus. Happily we are extraordinarily fortunate in having hardly any frontier line in all our vast empire, except where we border on barbarous tribes, and there our frontier is now thoroughly "scientific"! In the one important exception to this there is not the least apprehension of war.

Hence we are enabled to avoid the terrible drain upon our resources which would be occasioned by an overgrown standing army raised by conscription. We have, however, a special burden in our navy.

Neither we nor any other single nation can afford materially to reduce our armaments, in the midst of wars and rumours of wars, and whilst all our neighbours are armed to the teeth and bent upon increasing their armaments. But certainly it is the manifest duty and the dearest concern of this and of every other nation to do our utmost to preserve peace and security. For nations no less than for individuals the saying holds good, "Blessed are the peacemakers."

We as a nation have often thrown great weight into the cause of peace. We set a noble example of loyal submission to the verdict of arbitration under trying circumstances, and in spite of a suspicion of hardship in the decision.

But it is a very serious question whether of late years our policy has been peaceful—whether we have not by our selfish jealousy and our selfish fears acted as a disturbing element which has rendered peace difficult or impossible all over the world. If there be any truth in this indictment our national responsibility is indeed heavy, and we should do much to alleviate the sufferings of the whole world by pursuing a quieter and less aggressive course.

A year ago the word "reciprocity" was often heard, to express a highly fashionable nostrum for our distress. But we do not so often hear of it now ; most probably because the thing signified was so indefinite and unsubstantial, and that when its advocates attempted accurately to formulate their meaning they found the task an impossibility. Reciprocity merely meant protection justified as a retaliatory measure. Most Englishmen profess to be adherents of Free Trade, but too often they have a narrow and mercenary view of its advantages. They think that Free Trade is a gain to the nation that sells and a loss to the nation that buys. Universal Free Trade would no doubt be good for us, but the present system of free trade in imports, and heavy taxes on our exports, is, they think, a pure loss.

This is the fundamental fallacy which underlies all protectionist systems. Men do not see that import trade is a source of wealth no less than export trade, and that an import duty does more harm to the nation which levies it than to that on whose merchandise it is levied. It is of no use for us to say that "half a loaf is better than no bread" to men who believe that the half which we keep is a negative quantity, and that the half which is taken from us is the only good part of the bread.

Attention was called to the matter in the House of Lords last year, and it there found several advocates; but far the most important speech of the evening was Lord Beaconsfield's. His speech was not that of a thorough going Free Trader. On the contrary, he displayed a certain hankering after Protection; but he made it abundantly clear that in his opinion at least Free Trade is for this country a fixed policy which will never be changed. "Reciprocity" he dismissed as an idle "phantom" to which definite form cannot be given by its most ardent supporters. We need not therefore at present argue the question of Reciprocity at any length. It is a simple and sufficient answer to say that we have nothing to tax which would put serious pressure upon foreign nations. Far the greater part of our imports from abroad are food and raw materials. If we tax these we may certainly harm the countries which send them, but we should do much more serious harm to ourselves, whom we should necessarily exclude from foreign markets, and that, as we have seen, would be misery and death to us.

If we protect manufactured goods only, the consequences would be less serious, since the imports of these are not considerable in amount. But, for this very reason, our action would be futile, whilst it would be a cruel injustice to the agricultural classes, whose industry would be the only one unprotected, as well as to consumers in general.

The advocates of Reciprocity do not for the most part attempt to put their demands into definite shape; but when they do, the absurdity and confusion of thought involved becomes glaringly apparent. The clearest proposal I have met with is contained in an Article by Mr. Wallace, the eminent naturalist, in the *Contemporary Review* for March, 1879. He proposes that whatever tax any foreign country lays upon our goods, we should lay precisely the same on the imports of the " very same" goods from them. By this simple process of retaliation he seems to think that in some mysterious manner we should annihilate the effects of Protection, and put ourselves on the same footing as though there were no tariffs at all.

It does not occur to him that we do not export

and import the "very same" goods from and to the various countries, in whatever sense we are to understand the ambiguous words "very same." He does not explain what good it will do us if we can induce France to admit our wine free of duty, or if America shows herself equally generous in regard to British corn.

Such a system would certainly injure the few countries, such as Belgium, which really send us the same kinds of manufactured goods as we send them. But in most cases it would be wholly inoperative.

It is madness to expect to force Free Trade upon our neighbours by giving it up ourselves. If we were to recede from our old policy it would be regarded by every nation of the world as a confession that we, the pioneers of Free Trade, had discovered that it was a mistake; and certainly those who have been so slow to learn from our example would be still slower to learn from our apostasy.

Although we have no power to counterbalance the duties levied upon our exports, we could if we would, put an end to another violation of the principles of Free Trade, by a course of action which depends on our own will.

The trades of sugar growing and sugar refining are being ruined in England, not only by foreign duties, but also by foreign bounties which enable our rivals to sell their sugar in England below the cost of production, indemnifying themselves at the expense of their own tax-payers.

There is no doubt that in so doing they are making a present to the English consumer; but it is a present of no great value to him, whilst it is fatal to a thoroughly legitimate British industry, and it is given at the expense of the foreign tax-payers, as well as at the cost of much absolute waste.

With such a present we can afford to dispense; at any rate, a succession of Governments have shown this to be their opinion, by the frequent remonstrances which they have addressed to foreign Governments on the subject.

If we could impose on foreign sugar a duty exactly equivalent to the bounty it has received abroad, we should simply annihilate the effects of the bounty and restore a sort of virtual Free Trade. The foreign Government would be making a present to the English Government instead of to the English consumer. But no doubt they would soon cease to confer a bounty which would do no good to any of their own subjects.

This course of imposing a duty to countervail a foreign *bounty* on the *very same* article would bear only a most superficial resemblance to that of imposing a duty to retaliate for a foreign *duty* on another article, even though it be of the same kind.\* The scheme appears to be objectionable, not because in principle it involves any violation of the laws of Free Trade, when these are rightly understood, but because of the immense difficulties of detail which would attend its practical application. Unless our countervailing duty is to be protective, it must be different for every foreign country, and adjusted accurately to the amount of bounty conferred by that country. Moreover, the duty must be varied whenever the bounty is changed. We may infer the Cimmerian darkness in which the whole subject is wrapt, and the difficulty which the necessary adjustments would involve, when we find that the amount which the bounty costs France annually has been variously estimated from £80,000 to £1,000,000. Then there would be great difficulties in levying a differential duty, as it is not always easy to discover the real country of origin. We should besides find ourselves seriously hampered by our commercial treaties, which are, according to Lord Beaconsfield, more than thirty-eight in number. Besides this, we cannot afford to make any concession, even in appearance to Pro-

---

\* Mr. Wallace, as we hinted above, in his Article in the *Contemporary*, seems to fall into a hopeless confusion of language between the two senses of "very same," which sometimes in his Paper means identically the same, and sometimes only of the same description.

tection. England, like Cæsar's wife, must be above suspicion.

Bi-metallism seems of late to have won many adherents. The Liverpool Chamber of Commerce appointed a special committee of seventeen members to inquire into " The state of trade in connection with the discrediting of silver as money." They arrived unanimously at the conclusion that the present distress arose in very large measure from that cause, and that it would be possible to restore silver to its former value by " recognition of the two metals as full legal tender money" at a " fixed ratio," to be fixed by an agreement among the " leading monetary powers." A deputation waited upon the Chancellor of the Exchequer to urge these views upon him.

Now, undoubtedly the depreciation of silver is a most serious evil, threatening bankruptcy, or, at any rate, extreme financial difficulties to India and many other silver-using countries, besides causing the gravest inconvenience to trade by its violent fluctuations in degree. Any measure which would raise or steady the value of silver would be most useful.

It may well be doubted, however, whether any change in the price of the precious metals has such serious effects as many suppose. International trade is after all virtually barter, and the part which gold and silver play in it is of secondary importance.

India buys our cotton goods and our iron with raw cotton and jute, not with rupees. To the merchant who transacts the business it will matter little if he gets more rupees than usual for his cotton and iron, and less cotton and jute than usual for his rupees. It is only rapid fluctuations in value that will sometimes hurt him and sometimes help him; but on the whole will do much harm by introducing an unnecessary element of uncertainty into his business.

The case is different with old standing debts which must be paid in gold, or with fixed payments, such as salaries, pensions, and the like, which are received in India and spent in England. Here the result of depreciation is pure and unmitigated loss.

It is often supposed that the relative value of gold and silver depends upon causes out of the control of legislation, and that it would be as impossible to fix it arbitrarily as it has always proved to fix the price of bread.

But this view is not altogether correct. The value of these metals, as of other things, depends upon the establishment of an equilibrium between supply and demand. Now, the demand for the precious metals depends largely upon legislative action. We have seen that the cause of the present appreciation of gold and depreciation of silver is to be found in the action of the German Government, which has substituted gold for silver as the principal currency, and in that of the Latin Union which has practically followed its example, even more than in the enormous silver production of the mines of Nevada, and in the decreased and inadequate supply of gold from Australia and California.

If any State make both metals legal tender indifferently at a fixed ratio, the result is that if either metal be undervalued, with regard to the market value of the metals for the time being, it is (in accordance with "Gresham's Law") driven out of circulation in that country, and the currency will consist exclusively of the over-valued metal. Of course this, by creating an extra demand for the one metal and an overflow of the other, tends to bring both all over the world nearer to the fixed ratio.

If several countries which together employ a large fraction of the world's currency were to agree together to make gold and silver legal tender at some fixed ratio—the same, or anything like the same, as that which they bear spontaneously—there would be a strong tendency for them to remain automatically at that point. Supposing, for instance, England, America and the Latin Union agreed to fix the legal tender ratio at $15\frac{1}{2}$, and to allow unlimited coinage of both metals, every one who had debts to pay would instantly wish to buy silver and sell gold, and the inevitable result would be that silver would rise in price to that ratio. Then it would be indifferent to every one in these countries whether he paid his debts in gold or silver, and either metal would be used according to convenience. But if either fell in the least below the fixed ratio there would be so strong a demand for it, and the demand for the other metal would fall off so much in all countries where the ratio was fixed by law, that the conventional ratio would necessarily be restored.

This experiment has been tried in America as well as in France, and has tended, no doubt, to steady the oscillations of the two metals. But neither country held a large enough fraction of the world's coinage to make the ratio completely fixed, and the ratio chosen by America was not exactly the same as that of France; so that the former country, unable to make her ratio prevail over that of France, never had the advantage of a real double currency at all, but used at one time silver to the exclusion of gold, at another gold to the exclusion of silver.

When gold was overvalued in France, it was altogether driven out by silver; but although this must have somewhat lowered the value of gold and raised that of silver it was not a sufficiently powerful cause to bring them to the legal tender ratio. In like manner, when gold became depreciated it drove out the silver from France, and she, according to Chevallier, acted as a parachute to break the fall of gold. We may reasonably suppose that a more extensive confederation of States would act, not as a parachute, but like a balloon which trails a rope on the ground and so remains automatically at a fixed height.

Thus, a state of stable equilibrium in which the two metals should bear perpetually a ratio of value to one another, fixed by law, is not such an impossible dream as it at first sounds. On the contrary, it has been partially realized in the past, and probably will be again achieved in the near future.

It is a question for the metallurgist to decide whether there is more probability of a very rich new field of silver being opened up than of gold. Unless this be the case, it appears that, as Professor Jevons has pointed out,* a double standard of gold and silver would be less extreme in its com-

---

\* See Jevons' "Money," p. 138.

pounded oscillations of value, with respect to things in general, than a single gold standard.

Although we came to substitute a single gold standard in England for our ancient silver standard by a sort of accident, there is a general, although a vague, feeling in England that not only is the single gold standard the best of all possible standards, but that it is a part of the order of nature, and that any proposal to modify it is almost as dishonest, or at any rate quite as dangerous, as an attempt to repudiate the National Debt.

Our intense shrinking from change, unless the change be very clearly proved to be for the better, and our slowness to see that it is for the better, is, on the whole, one of the most valuable qualities of the English race; but it is often almost as great an obstacle to reform as it is to dangerous innovation.

But if we could deal with our monetary system unfettered by national prejudice, it would not be difficult to devise arrangements which, although in principle complicated, would be simple enough in practice, and would answer all the ends of money better than the somewhat rude system which we have at present.

There are two main requisites for a good system of currency. The standard of value should be invariable, or as nearly so as in the nature of things is possible, and the money should be convenient for the ordinary business of buying and selling and the like.

The first object would be best attained if we, in common with a sufficient number of other nations, constituted gold and silver indifferently our standard legal tender money, at some convenient fixed ratio. Provided this were done on a large enough scale, it would be almost impossible for either metal to deviate much from the ratio.

But one great disadvantage of this double standard system is that the very machinery by which uniformity of ratio is secured is an alternate disappearance from the circulation of the country of whichever metal is for the moment undervalued.

Now, with our present arrangements of currency, we could not dispense either with gold or silver in the transactions of every-day life without extreme inconvenience.

This difficulty would be avoided if we reintroduced £1 bank notes, which are a more convenient medium of circulation than sovereigns; and if besides our standard silver coins—which might be crowns, or whatever other large coin is most convenient—we used, as at present, small silver coins of nominal value exceeding their real value, and only legal tender to a limited point.

Then silver and paper would be our ordinary currency; neither of which could possibly be driven out of circulation, and it would be a matter of indifference to us whether gold or silver were for the moment the prevailing standard.

But at present there would be serious difficulty and inconvenience in introducing a double standard. The tendency has been of late in the opposite direction; it has seemed that all the most civilized nations of the world would become chrysomono-metallic, and it will not be easy to turn back the current.

The present ratio of gold to silver* is 18 instead of the old 15½. If the ratio were to be fixed by convention it would have to be at 15½ or at some point much nearer to that than to 18. Those who are interested in silver would not be content to have the present ratio stereotyped.

But if the old ratio or anything like it were chosen, the market value of the two metals could only be brought into accordance with the fixed ratio and kept there, by an extensive revolution and a general substitution of the use of silver for gold.

We may hope, however, that the approaching exhaustion of the silver mines of Nevada, and the promised opening of a new and rich gold field in

---

* March 15, 1880, silver at 51 13⁄16 d.

India will tend to restore to silver its old value in relation to gold. If this be brought about, not only will it be a great relief to the finances of India, but it will also make the way clear for bi-metallism.

In the meanwhile any artificial rehabilitation of silver must be at the expense of gold which would be extensively thrown out of circulation, and consequently depreciated all over the world.

Now, we in England have a wholesome horror of any voluntary action which can affect the standard of value. It savours too much of sharp practice and even of repudiation. Hence we most justly shrink from a measure which would certainly injure creditors and benefit debtors.

No doubt in one sense depreciation of gold, or, in other words, a general rise of prices, would benefit trade. It would have the reverse effect to that which we traced in the case of a general fall in prices, and would enable the capitalist to get a larger share of the produce of labour, whilst the labourers' money wages would rise.

Thus every one would appear to be better off and the approaching inflation of trade would be hastened and increased. But the prosperity which depends merely upon the value of money can have no reality. It is built on a foundation of sand, and cannot bring us true wealth. What one man gains another loses, and although every one may seem to be growing rich, much of the wealth which men acquire is a fairy gold which soon withers away to worthless ashes. It is not by changes such as this that we can reap solid wealth, but by Hard Work, Free Trade, Honesty.

THE END.

www.ingramcontent.com/pod-product-compliance
Lightning Source LLC
Chambersburg PA
CBHW030906170426
43193CB00009BA/747